COMPACT *Research*

Epilepsy

Diseases and Disorders

ReferencePoint
Press®

San Diego, CA

Select* books in the Compact Research series include:

Current Issues
Abortion
Animal Experimentation
Biomedical Ethics
Cloning
Conflict in the Middle East
The Death Penalty
Energy Alternatives
Free Speech
Genetic Engineering
Global Warming and
   Climate Change
Gun Control
Illegal Immigration

Islam
Media Violence
National Security
Nuclear Weapons and
   Security
Obesity
School Violence
Stem Cells
Terrorist Attacks
U.S. Border Control
Video Games
World Energy Crisis

Diseases and Disorders
ADHD
Alzheimer's Disease
Anorexia
Autism
Bipolar Disorders
Hepatitis

HPV
Meningitis
Phobias
Sexually Transmitted
   Diseases

Drugs
Alcohol
Antidepressants
Club Drugs
Cocaine and Crack
Hallucinogens
Heroin
Inhalants

Marijuana
Methamphetamine
Nicotine and Tobacco
Performance-Enhancing
   Drugs
Prescription Drugs
Steroids

Energy and the Environment
Biofuels
Deforestation
Hydrogen Power

Solar Power
Wind Power

*For a complete list of titles please visit www.referencepointpress.com.

Epilepsy

by Peggy J. Parks

Contents

Foreword

"Where is the knowledge we have lost in information?"

—T.S. Eliot, "The Rock."

As modern civilization continues to evolve, its ability to create, store, distribute, and access information expands exponentially. The explosion of information from all media continues to increase at a phenomenal rate. By 2020 some experts predict the worldwide information base will double every 73 days. While access to diverse sources of information and perspectives is paramount to any democratic society, information alone cannot help people gain knowledge and understanding. Information must be organized and presented clearly and succinctly in order to be understood. The challenge in the digital age becomes not the creation of information, but how best to sort, organize, enhance, and present information.

ReferencePoint Press developed the *Compact Research* series with this challenge of the information age in mind. More than any other subject area today, researching current issues can yield vast, diverse, and unqualified information that can be intimidating and overwhelming for even the most advanced and motivated researcher. The *Compact Research* series offers a compact, relevant, intelligent, and conveniently organized collection of information covering a variety of current topics ranging from illegal immigration and deforestation to diseases such as anorexia and meningitis.

The series focuses on three types of information: objective single-author narratives, opinion-based primary source quotations, and facts and statistics. The clearly written objective narratives provide context and reliable background information. Primary source quotes are carefully selected and cited, exposing the reader to differing points of view. And facts and statistics sections aid the reader in evaluating perspectives. Presenting these key types of information creates a richer, more balanced learning experience.

For better understanding and convenience, the series enhances information by organizing it into narrower topics and adding design features that make it easy for a reader to identify desired content. For example, in *Compact Research: Illegal Immigration*, a chapter covering the economic impact of illegal immigration has an objective narrative explaining the various ways the economy is impacted, a balanced section of numerous primary source quotes on the topic, followed by facts and full-color illustrations to encourage evaluation of contrasting perspectives.

The ancient Roman philosopher Lucius Annaeus Seneca wrote, "It is quality rather than quantity that matters." More than just a collection of content, the *Compact Research* series is simply committed to creating, finding, organizing, and presenting the most relevant and appropriate amount of information on a current topic in a user-friendly style that invites, intrigues, and fosters understanding.

Epilepsy at a Glance

Epilepsy Defined

Epilepsy is part of a large, diverse group of disorders that all involve recurrent seizures that occur because brain cells (neurons) send abnormal signals to other neurons, glands, and muscles in the body.

Causes

In most cases of epilepsy there is no known cause. In some cases genetics, head injury, brain tumors, alcoholism, damage to a fetus's brain before or during birth, and poisoning by toxic substances such as lead or mercury may be contributing factors.

Prevalence

The World Health Organization states that approximately 50 million people throughout the world suffer from epilepsy. In the United States, as many as 3 million people have the disorder.

Diagnosis

A person is thought to have epilepsy if he or she has suffered two or more seizures not caused by some unknown medical condition. Physicians diagnose the disorder though physical examinations, blood tests, and brain scans such as electroencephalograms (EEGs) or magnetic resonance imaging (MRI).

Risks

Because of seizures, people with epilepsy risk injuries from falling, burns, and crashes while driving or riding a bicycle, as well as drowning. Two of the greatest risks are status epilepticus (prolonged seizures that can lead to brain damage) and sudden unexplained death in epilepsy.

Preventive Measures

Although epilepsy cannot necessarily be prevented, people can lessen risks by wearing helmets while riding bicycles or playing sports, wearing seat belts and shoulder harnesses in vehicles, and buckling children in cars seats. Pregnant women must avoid drugs, alcohol, and smoking and must get proper prenatal care.

Progress Toward a Cure

Epilepsy is a neurological condition, so it cannot be cured in the same way that antibiotics cure infectious diseases. But medical science has resulted in the development of numerous anticonvulsive drugs and surgical techniques that allow many people with epilepsy either to be seizure free or to suffer markedly fewer seizures.

Overview

❝Epilepsy is not a 'one size fits all problem.' It can look, feel and act differently in different people.❞

—Orrin Devinsky, director of the New York University Comprehensive Epilepsy Center.

❝Few experiences match the drama of a convulsive seizure. . . . Within minutes, the attack is over, and the person regains consciousness but is exhausted and dazed.❞

—National Institute of Neurological Disorders and Stroke, an organization whose mission is to reduce the burden of neurological disease.

Dan Wheeless had his first seizure at the beginning of eighth grade. With no warning he collapsed in the school hallway, writhing on the floor and jerking his arms and legs uncontrollably. When the seizure ended, he felt exhausted and had no memory of what had happened. Because he was known as the class clown, his friends assumed he was just performing one of his usual antics. "People thought I was just joking around," he says, "wriggling around on the floor, so they were kicking me and saying, 'Okay Dan, get up, whatever.'"[1]

Wheeless was later diagnosed with epilepsy, and now, at the age of 32, he still suffers from intermittent seizures. About 50 percent of the time he can foresee when one is about to occur because he has trouble processing information that he would normally find simple. He describes what happens when he has a seizure: "I'm out for 15 minutes, maybe longer. The violent jerking is probably a minute, or 2 minutes, followed by heavy breathing—it's like a scream, it's all the muscles contracting and all the air being forced out of my lungs."[2]

In the moments just after he wakes up, Wheeless says, he does not remember having the seizure, nor does he recall who he is or who other people are. Although he is not seizure free, medications have cut the number of episodes to about 4 per year. "That's fantastic," he says, "compared to someone who's having 20 an hour, or 20 a day, which is completely debilitating. Somebody who has to wear a helmet, and be stuck in a wheelchair, and has really lost everything. I'm lucky to have the kind of epilepsy that I have. . . . It's scary, yeah, but thank God, thank God it's only—it can be controlled."[3]

What Is Epilepsy?

Epilepsy is not a single disorder, but rather is part of a large, diverse group of disorders that are sometimes referred to as epilepsies or epilepsy syndromes. Although scientists have identified numerous types, the commonality among all is the tendency to cause recurrent seizures, or a sudden, involuntary movement of muscles. Because of that, the word *epilepsy* is a fitting name because it is derived from the Greek word *epilambanein*, which means the condition of being overcome, seized, or attacked. Seizures vary in severity from a dazed state that involves slight muscle twitching and eye blinking, to severe seizures whereby the person loses consciousness, drops to the ground, and has violent convulsions.

In order to understand why someone who has epilepsy suffers from seizures, it is important to be aware of how the brain functions. The human body runs on electricity, as investigative journalist and epilepsy sufferer Joshua Kors explains: "A steady current from the brain makes the eyes see, the lungs breathe and all the other organs function. Microscopic cells in the brain known as neurons produce this electrical charge. When one neuron fires its charge, nearby neurons are

> " Epilepsy is not a single disorder, but rather is part of a large, diverse group of disorders that are sometimes referred to as epilepsies or epilepsy syndromes. "

> **Epilepsy affects people of all races, walks of life, and ages, although an estimated 50 percent of cases are diagnosed in childhood or adolescence.**

prompted to do the same, triggering a sequence of cell firings that sends a coordinated message to the rest of the body." That is not the case, however, with people who have epilepsy. Their brains contain neurons that disrupt the normal electrical transmission and go "haywire," as Kors writes: "These neurons are instigators of an electrical riot. When one fires at random, nearby brain cells begin firing erratically as well. Together, these wild electrical pulses send a frazzled message to the body, resulting in a seizure. . . . Seizures grow more intense as neurons that are behaving properly get recruited by the rebellion and begin to fire at random."[4]

Who Suffers from Epilepsy?

Epilepsy affects people of all races, walks of life, and ages, although an estimated 50 percent of cases are diagnosed in childhood or adolescence. According to the World Health Organization (WHO), approximately 50 million people throughout the world have epilepsy. In the United States, health officials estimate that 2.5 million to 3 million people suffer from epilepsy, with about 200,000 new cases being reported each year. Although researchers do not understand why, males have a slightly higher chance of developing epilepsy than females.

Warning Signs

The first sign of epilepsy is the onset of a seizure, although having one does not necessarily indicate that the person has the disorder. Only after someone has had two or more seizures is epilepsy suspected, and the diagnosis can be confirmed with an electroencephalogram (EEG), or brain scan. The National Institute of Neurological Disorders and Stroke (NINDS) states that health professionals have identified more than 30 different types of seizures, which are divided into two major categories: focal and generalized. The difference between them is that focal seizures

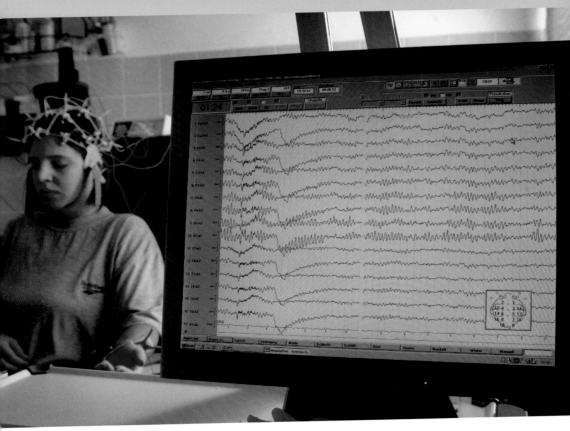

A patient undergoes an electroencephalogram (EEG), a test used to diagnose epilepsy. During an EEG, special sensors, or electrodes, are attached to the patient's head and hooked by wires to a computer. The computer measures and records electrical activity in the brain, as shown by the wavy lines on the computer screen.

originate in only one part of the brain, whereas the entire brain is involved in generalized seizures. People with epilepsy may suffer from just one type of seizure or more than one.

During a simple focal seizure, the person remains conscious but experiences unusual feelings and sensations, such as unexplainable euphoria, anger, or sadness. He or she may also hear, see, smell, or feel things that are not actually real. Someone who has a complex focal seizure has a change in consciousness, such as being in a dreamlike state, or loses consciousness altogether.

The seizures in the generalized category are the most serious, as well as the most dangerous for the person who suffers from them. For instance, tonic-clonic seizures (often called grand mal seizures) typically result in violent, uncontrollable convulsive movements. People who have these types of seizures often cry out and then lose consciousness; their eyes roll back in their heads; their bodies stiffen; their arms, legs, and hands begin jerking spasmodically; and they often drool and lose control of their bladder and/or bowels. Such seizures can last anywhere from a few minutes to a half hour, sometimes longer. On many occasions, a person who has experienced this type of seizure wakes up feeling confused and exhausted, with no memory of what happened.

> " **Before having a seizure many people experience what is known as an aura, meaning unusual sensations that warn of an impending seizure.** "

Before having a seizure many people experience what is known as an aura, meaning unusual sensations that warn of an impending seizure. This is the case with Kors, who was diagnosed with epilepsy when he was 13 years old. At one point in his life, he suffered six or seven seizures per day, and he always knew when a seizure was going to overtake his body, as he explains: "Each began as a small neural misfire: a red light that would burst into the upper-right-hand corner of my vision. Most times the light would fade. Other times it spread, as if my field of vision had caught on fire."[5]

What Causes Epilepsy?

According to the WHO, with most cases of epilepsy, no cause is apparent. This is known as idiopathic epilepsy, and the WHO states that it affects 6 out of 10 people with the disorder. When there is a known cause, it is referred to as symptomatic epilepsy, and if there is a likely cause, it is called cryptogenic epilepsy. Basically, anything that disturbs normal neuron activity can be a possible cause of epilepsy, as the NINDS explains:

> Epilepsy may develop because of an abnormality in brain wiring, an imbalance of nerve signaling chemicals called

neurotransmitters, or some combination of these factors. Researchers believe that some people with epilepsy have an abnormally high level of *excitatory neurotransmitters* that increase neuronal activity, while others have an abnormally low level of *inhibitory neurotransmitters* that decrease neuronal activity in the brain. Either situation can result in too much neuronal activity and cause epilepsy.[6]

Potential contributors to the development of epilepsy include genetic abnormalities, brain damage caused by severe blows to the head, and brain tumors. Other possible causes are infection of the brain, excessive use of alcohol, injury to a fetus's brain before or during birth, and poisoning by toxic substances such as lead or mercury.

Diagnosis and Treatment

When epilepsy is suspected, physicians take a complete medical history and perform a physical examination, as well as blood tests. It is also common for tests such as EEGs, which measure and record the electrical activity in the brain, to be performed. Other typical brain-scan tests include computed axial tomography (CAT) and magnetic resonance imaging (MRI), both of which reveal the structure of the brain and can indicate abnormalities.

Epilepsy is often successfully treated with prescription medications, and many people who take the drugs see a marked reduction in seizures. Some even become completely seizure free over time. This has not been the case with Lydia Thompson, however, for whom medications have not helped curb seizures. Lydia, who is 15 years old, has had seizures nearly every day since she was a toddler. Her mother, Cynthia Folio, explains: "She wakes up nearly every morning to a couple

> " **Seizures are highly unpredictable, and in many cases they occur for no apparent reason.** "

of seizures and also sometimes has them during the day. . . . She also has 'cluster' seizures every few days, where intervention is required to stop them or they would continue indefinitely."[7]

Some people who have tried to take antiepileptic medications found that even though they helped stop or slow down seizures, the drugs affected them physically in ways that were unbearable. Serious side effects have been associated with some of these drugs, including dizziness, lethargy, nausea, hyperactivity, and mental confusion, among others. New York University epilepsy specialist Orrin Devinsky says that when patients take these medications, they have to balance the unpleasantness of seizures with the misery of other symptoms. He explains:

> You might have two staring spells a month lasting a couple of minutes, and you're on a high dose of medication. Now, I can put you on a second medication and get you down to one a month. So now you've got two extra minutes a month but in exchange it's affecting your quality of life for the 15 hours a day you're awake: it may make you tired, or dizzy, or cause mood changes or memory problems. So do you want to make that trade-off?[8]

For those who cannot control seizures by taking medication, brain surgery may be warranted. That is only possible, however, for people who suffer from localized epilepsy, meaning the disease originates in just one portion of the brain. If that is the case, physicians can use brain imaging technology to pinpoint the exact section, and then surgically remove it.

In lieu of surgery, some people with epilepsy undergo vagus nerve stimulation (VNS), which involves surgically implanting a small, battery-powered device underneath the skin of the chest. During the procedure a surgeon threads a plastic tube under the skin and attaches it to the vagus nerve, a large nerve in the neck that acts as a major connection between the brain and the rest of the body. Then the device is programmed to deliver small jolts of electricity to the vagus nerve every few minutes. Although scientists are not sure why, VNS therapy has been shown to reduce seizures in some epilepsy sufferers by up to 40 percent.

What Triggers Seizures?

Seizures are highly unpredictable, and in many cases they occur for no apparent reason. People who have epilepsy have to be careful to get enough sleep, avoid smoking or drinking alcohol to excess, watch their diets, and maintain healthy lifestyles, because taking those precautions will lessen the risk of having seizures. Devinsky often cautions young people in their teens and twenties who have epilepsy that they cannot afford to be reckless by forgetting to take their medications and staying up all night doing homework or partying with their friends—he has lost more than 150 young patients for that very reason. "I had a patient who hadn't had a seizure in two years," he says. "Last fall I got a call. He went off to college, stayed up late one night at a party and never got up the next morning."[9]

Exactly what triggers someone to have a seizure depends on the type of epilepsy the person has. For those who have one of the reflex epilepsy types, which affect about 6 percent of epilepsy sufferers, seizures can be triggered by visual or auditory stimuli. For instance, someone with photosensitive epilepsy may have seizures when exposed to flashing lights, complex visual patterns, the subtly flickering light of a computer screen, or the chaotic on-screen action of video games. An individual with musicogenic epilepsy can suffer seizures when hearing certain types of music. This was the case with Stacey Gayle, who is 1 of only 100 people known to have this rare type of epilepsy. When she was 21 years old, Gayle had 2 tonic-clonic seizures in one night. Doctors diagnosed her with epilepsy, although they did not know what type it was. Then she was at a barbecue with some friends, and when a rap song called "Temperature" began to play, she immediately went into a seizure. "Several weeks later," she writes, "I almost fell overboard on a boat because I seized as the same song came on. Soon, I realized it was happening with several different kinds of music." This was extremely difficult for her, as she explains: "I couldn't go to church, Christmas parties, or the mall. I had to quit my job because of people's cell-phone ring tones. I felt so isolated."[10] In February 2007 tests showed which area of Gayle's brain was affected, and she underwent surgery so doctors could remove the problem section. Since that time she has been seizure free.

> " Because seizures can occur at any time of the day or night, people with epilepsy are constantly at risk for accidents and injury. "

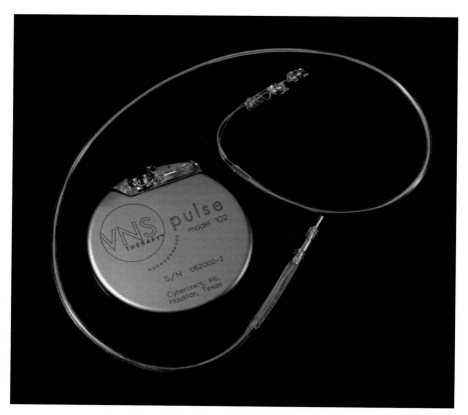

Vagus nerve stimulation devices, like the one pictured here, are designed to prevent seizures. They operate something like a pacemaker, sending regular, mild pulses of electrical energy to the brain. The device is placed under the skin on the chest wall and a wire runs from it to the vagus nerve in the neck.

What Are the Risks Associated with Epilepsy?

Because seizures can occur at any time of the day or night, people with epilepsy are constantly at risk for accidents and injury. Folio explains how this affects her daughter, Lydia: "Lately, she has experienced seizures that come with no warning and make her fall down, sometimes causing her to hurt herself. She has to wear a helmet much of the time."[11] Drowning is also a higher risk for those with epilepsy. Studies have shown that people with epilepsy are as much as 20 times more likely to die of drowning than those who do not have the disorder. Another potential risk is for women with epilepsy who become pregnant, of whom about 25 to 40 percent experience an increase in seizures. Although the risk is small, there is also the chance of having a baby born with birth defects if the mother takes epilepsy medications while she is pregnant.

According to the NINDS, the greatest risks for people who have epilepsy stem from 2 life-threatening conditions: status epilepticus and sudden unexplained death in epilepsy (SUDEP). Status epilepticus is a condition in which an individual either has an abnormally long seizure (lasting more than 5 or 10 minutes) or has a series of seizures without regaining consciousness in between. The NINDS states that nearly 200,000 people develop this disorder each year in the United States, resulting in about 42,000 deaths. Those who survive may sustain brain damage from the prolonged seizures. A study that was published by Canadian researchers in 2007 described a man who had status epilepticus for 48 hours, and this led to serious, irreversible damage in the right hemisphere of his brain.

Sudden unexplained death in epilepsy is a mystery to scientists. For reasons that are unknown, people with epilepsy have an increased risk of dying suddenly and unexpectedly. The Centers for Disease Control and Prevention (CDC) states that SUDEP usually occurs in people between the ages of 20 and 40, although it can affect people of all ages, and accounts for 2 to 17 percent of deaths in the United States each year. Henry Foster Lapham was a victim of SUDEP in February 2008. He was just 4 years old when he was diagnosed with epilepsy, and not long afterward he had a seizure during the night and died in his sleep.

How Epilepsy Affects Daily Life

Although people with epilepsy often lead happy, fulfilling lives, many face challenges such as the frustration of not being able to drive or participate in certain recreational activities because of the risk of seizure. Kevin Eggers is a 20-year-old college student who was diagnosed with epilepsy when he was 16. Medication has curbed his seizures to only 1 every 6 months, but he went through a rough time when he was in high school, as he explains: "My epilepsy was at its peak in severity when I was trying to live my high school years to the fullest. I loved school, I loved soccer, and I loved the ability to use my new driver's license, but because of my epilepsy, these aspects of my life were restricted. And the car I was restoring with my dad . . . sat in the driveway taunting me."[12] Eggers says that he had formerly been a starting player on the soccer team, but once he started having seizures, he was benched for most of the games. He also had to give up his hobby of cross-country running for fear that he would have a seizure when he was alone on a training run.

A quality-of-life study published in October 2007 involved thousands of people from California who suffer from epilepsy. One finding was that 36 percent of respondents said they were physically disabled or unable to work, compared to 5 percent of adults without the disorder. Participants who had recent seizures reported suffering from impaired physical or mental health for 9 to 12 days in the past month, compared to only 2 to 4 days for those without the disorder. Another finding was that people with epilepsy were more likely to be unemployed, live in lower-income households, and engage in unhealthy behaviors such as smoking. "As with other chronic diseases," the study authors explain, "epilepsy takes a toll on physical and mental health, including interfering with daily activities."[13]

According to the CDC, in some cases epilepsy may be preventable. For instance, one precaution is wearing helmets to reduce the risk of head injury associated with a bicycle or motorcycle accident, as well as contact sports such as hockey or football. Another important precaution is wearing seat belts and shoulder harnesses and securely buckling children into car seats to protect against head injury in the event of motor vehicle accidents. Other precautionary measures include not smoking, avoiding excessive use of alcohol, good prenatal care for pregnant women, and avoiding exposure to lead and other toxic substances.

Can Epilepsy Be Cured?

Scientists have made excellent progress in gaining a better understanding of epilepsy and its possible causes, as well as in developing numerous drugs that can help control seizures. And some people, such as Stacey Gayle, have essentially been cured by brain surgery and are now seizure free. The good news for children who have epilepsy is that many outgrow the disorder by the time they are adults. In one type, known as benign rolandic epilepsy, nearly all children outgrow the epilepsy and are seizure free by the time they reach puberty. However, many continue to suffer from this debilitating neurological disorder, and much remains unknown. The NINDS states that "while research has led to many advances in understanding and treating epilepsy, there are many unanswered questions."[14] As research continues, those questions may be answered in the near future.

What Is Epilepsy?

66 **Living with epilepsy can . . . be like a roller coaster ride. At times, life is stable and you feel that you're coping well. Then other times life throws you a curve and things just don't work out the way you expect.** 99

—Patricia O. Shafer, an epilepsy nurse specialist, and Andres M. Kanner, professor of neurological sciences, at Chicago's Rush Medical College.

66 **Depending on the part of the brain affected, seizures can produce hallucinations, anxiety, feelings of religious ecstasy or bizarre psychological tics such as 'hyperfamiliarity,' a delusional sense that you're already acquainted with everyone you meet.** 99

—Jerry Adler, senior editor of *Newsweek* magazine, and Eliza Gray, a contributing writer.

For thousands of years humans have been aware of the disorder known as epilepsy, but it was not at all understood. Epilepsy was long considered to be mysterious and frightening, and people who suffered from it were believed to be possessed by the devil. Babylonian tablets dating as far back as 1067 B.C. describe different types of seizures, each of which was associated with the name of a god or spirit (usually evil). These ancient documents emphasized that seizures were of a supernatural cause and likely a sign of demonic possession. This continued to be the prevailing belief until 400 B.C., when the Greek physician Hippocrates released the first book about epilepsy, titled *On the Sacred Disease.* Hippocrates refuted the idea that epilepsy was caused by possession by the devil and said it was a disorder of the brain that was due to natural causes. He wrote: "It is thus with regard to the disease called Sacred: It appears to me to be nowise more divine nor more sacred than other diseases, but has a natural cause like other affections."[15] Hippocrates and his followers believed that epilepsy was a hereditary disorder that tended to run in families. They believed that epilepsy was somehow connected to blockages in the blood vessels to the brain, a belief later shown to be incorrect.

A Broader Understanding of Epilepsy

During the late-nineteenth century, British neurologist John Hughlings Jackson became well known for his contributions toward a broader understanding of epilepsy. He spent 40 years studying the disorder, including observing seizures suffered by his wife. In his 1870 essay "A Study of Convulsions," Jackson stated than an epileptic seizure was a symptom rather than a disease in and of itself. He added that when someone suffered a seizure, this implied "only that there is an occasional, an excessive, and a disorderly discharge of nerve tissue on muscles. This discharge occurs in all degrees; it occurs with all sorts of conditions of ill health, at all ages, and under innumerable circumstances."[16]

> " **Epilepsy was long considered to be mysterious and frightening, and people who suffered from it were believed to be possessed by the devil.** "

Jackson's mention of "disorderly discharge" referred to his belief that seizures were caused by electrical charges that started at one point in the brain and radiated out from there. Because seizures affected different types of body movements, he inferred that the brain was divided into different sections, with each section controlling the movement of a particular body part. In his writings, he described the particular part of the brain where he believed most seizures originated, the cerebral cortex area. In 1873 he offered a description of epilepsy as an "occasional, sudden, excessive and rapid discharge of gray matter of some part of the brain."[17]

In his later writings Jackson described what he called the "dreamy state," which involved different levels of consciousness associated with epilepsy. He addressed the issue of auras that people experienced before having a seizure, writing: "The so-called 'intellectual aura' (I call it a 'dreamy state') is a striking symptom. This is a very elaborate or 'voluminous' mental state." Jackson cited many examples of how the dreamy state affected various patients. The mildest stage was the first degree of consciousness, when a person experienced misperceptions of reality, fuzzy memory, and/or mild delirium. On the opposite end of the spectrum was the third degree of consciousness, characterized by seizures that involved struggling, kicking, and shouting that was "often taken for hysteria." Jackson added that during the process of having severe seizures, some patients became "violently maniacal."[18]

> " In his later writings Jackson described what he called the 'dreamy state,' which involved different levels of consciousness associated with epilepsy. "

Jackson's theories became highly influential among scientists who studied epilepsy, and his prolific research helped broaden their understanding of the disorder. His studies of the human brain and its connection with epilepsy earned him the title of the Father of English Neurology (neurology being the branch of medical science that relates to the study of the brain).

Epilepsy Syndromes

Although epilepsy is still considered to be a mysterious disorder, scientists now know it is a neurological condition that stems from disturbances in the brain's normal electrical functions. When clusters of neurons misfire, this causes abnormal signals to be sent to other neurons, glands, and muscles that are responsible for producing thoughts, awareness, feelings, actions, and control of bodily functions. The National Institute of Neurological Disorders and Stroke states that the normal pattern of neuronal activity becomes disrupted in people with epilepsy, which causes them to experience strange sensations, emotions, and behaviors. "During a seizure," says the NINDS, "neurons may fire as many as 500 times a second, much faster than normal. In some people, this happens only occasionally;

for others, it may happen up to hundreds of times a day."[19]

According to the NINDS, doctors have identified hundreds of epilepsy syndromes that are characterized by their symptoms or where they originate in the brain. One type is known as infantile spasms, which are clusters of seizures that usually begin in babies between the ages of 4 and 8 months old. These seizures often involve bending forward or the arching of the back, stiffening of the arms and legs, and sometimes violent jerking. The NINDS says that the seizures may occur in clusters of up to 100 spasms at a time, and many babies have several hundred seizures per day. This type of epilepsy is rare, and many children who suffer from it grow out of it by the time they are 5 years old. It can be devastating, however, because the disorder usually leaves permanent damage. A little girl named Abigail Shuckrow started having seizures when she was 2 months old, sometimes suffering 100 or more per day. This stopped her development and caused severe mental and physical impairments. As a result, Abigail is permanently blind, and doctors say that she will never be able to walk or talk.

> **The NINDS says that the seizures [of infantile spasms epilepsy] may occur in clusters of up to 100 spasms at a time, and many babies have several hundred seizures per day.**

Another rare but severe type of epilepsy is Lennox-Gastaut syndrome, which involves multiple seizure types and usually develops before a child is 4 years old. The most common seizures suffered by those who have the disorder are the severe tonic-clonic types, whereby they lose consciousness, their bodies stiffen up, and they shudder uncontrollably. Because of the seriousness of the seizures, as well as the frequency, children who suffer from Lennox-Gastaut syndrome are highly prone to injury and often must wear helmets to protect their heads. Some who have the disorder may go through periods of being seizure free, but most experience seizures for their entire lives, and in many cases medications do not help. One mother shares her story on the Epilepsy Therapy Project's Web site: "Kathy has been on every medication, many of them three or four times. Nothing has ever controlled the seizures well. As the doctors kept going up on the doses, she would either undergo terrible personality changes, turn into a zombie, or look drunk. We have finally come to accept the seizures and her mental handicaps."[20]

One of the most common forms of epilepsy is known as absence epilepsy, which almost always develops during childhood or adolescence. It typically involves mild seizures that are often not noticeable to others. For instance, people with this disorder may go into a dazed state, rapidly blink their eyes, and/or jerk one or both arms. When the seizure ends, they can resume whatever they were doing without feeling any aftereffects. Sue Nowak (not her real name) observed a case of absence epilepsy with one of her friends when she was in high school, as she explains:

> **Another rare but severe type of epilepsy is Lennox-Gastaut syndrome, which involves multiple seizure types and usually develops before a child is 4 years old.**

> We never knew when it was going to happen or why, but we'd be talking and laughing with Tammi when all of a sudden she'd get perfectly still, not moving a muscle, staring off into space and blinking her eyes. We had no idea what was wrong and we'd snap our fingers in front of her face and say, "Tammi! Tammi!" but it was like she couldn't hear or see us, she just kept staring straight ahead and blinking. And then she'd come out of it, look a little confused, and start talking and laughing again like nothing had happened. It was spooky.[21]

Nowak says that at times this was frightening for her and her friends because they feared for Tammi. Nowak explains:

> She was a varsity cheerleader, and I think she kept her epilepsy hidden from the coaches or she probably wouldn't have made the squad. One time she was out cheering

on the field and she had a seizure—she just stood there, staring straight ahead, while all the other girls were doing flips and jumps around her. I was scared to death that she was going to get hurt. I used to beg her not to climb up and do the pyramid, but she wouldn't listen. Fortunately, nothing bad ever happened to her and I think she eventually grew out of it.[22]

Depending on the type of epilepsy children have, many grow out of it. Estimates range from 50 to 60 percent who outgrow it by the time they reach puberty or adulthood, although with some types, the number is much higher. For instance, according to the Epilepsy Foundation, 95 percent of children who have benign rolandic epilepsy outgrow their seizures by the time they are 15.

When Warning Signs Are Subtle

With most cases of epilepsy, the disorder becomes obvious because someone has 2 or more seizures. But there are people whose symptoms go unnoticed for a number of years before the diagnosis is made. Marta (not her real name), a woman from Southern California, says that she and her husband had no idea their son Joshua had epilepsy until he was 9 years old. He had exhibited symptoms from the time he was 3 or 4, but they were very subtle and not obvious to anyone but his parents. Marta and her husband noticed that every once in a while, Joshua's body would shiver for a few seconds, as she explains: "In those moments everything froze. And it was very subtle. . . . If he was holding a pencil, he'd still be holding the pencil. If he was holding a fork at dinner, he would keep his hold on his fork. Nothing dropped. Nothing changed. It was as if he was just frozen for a moment in time, except that his body went through a little shiver."[23]

> **According to the doctor, the shivers that Joshua had experienced on and off throughout the years were actually mild seizures.**

Marta says that Joshua's shivering spells continued over a period of years, but they did not occur every day or even every week. Then during the summer before he entered fourth grade, he suffered a major seizure while playing with his Game Boy. "I was getting ready for work," she writes. "Suddenly I heard my husband yelling for me. I ran into the living room and Joshua was lying on the couch—unconscious, his lips turning blue. I called 911. By time the ambulance got there (which seemed like forever but I'm sure it was only a couple/few minutes) Joshua was breathing and partly conscious." Marta says that the ambulance took her son to the hospital, and after a variety of tests, everything seemed to be all right. On the advice of their doctor, Marta scheduled Joshua for an EEG as well as an appointment to see a pediatric neurologist—but before the day of the appointment arrived, he had another seizure. "He'd fallen off the chair," she says, "and this time we both saw him convulsing. When the seizure stopped, we carried him to his bed. He slept for a short while but when he woke up he complained of a terrible headache."[24]

When the family met with the pediatric neurologist, they learned that Joshua's EEG results confirmed that he had epilepsy. According to the doctor, the shivers that Joshua had experienced on and off throughout the years were actually mild seizures. Joshua was put on antiepileptic medication, and after being seizure free for a year and a half, he underwent another EEG that came back normal. The doctor gradually reduced the dosage of his medications, and about two years from the day Joshua had his first severe seizure, he was able to stop taking the drugs altogether. "He's one of the fortunate ones," says Marta. "Many people have to take medications their whole life in order to keep seizures under control, but Josh grew out of his epilepsy. He—and we—were very lucky."[25]

Looking Toward the Future

Since 400 B.C., when Hippocrates introduced the theory that epilepsy originated in the brain, scientists have gained a tremendous amount of knowledge about its relationship to neuronal activity. They have identified hundreds of different epilepsy syndromes and developed numerous medications that help people control seizures. As research continues, medical science will undoubtedly reveal more about this mysterious disorder that affects tens of millions of people throughout the world—and that means there is hope in the future for those who suffer from it.

Primary Source Quotes*

What Is Epilepsy?

66**Epilepsy is characterized by unprovoked, recurring seizures that disrupt the nervous system and can cause mental and physical dysfunction.**99

—University of Maryland Medical Center, "Epilepsy—Introduction," December 31, 2007. www.umm.edu.

The University of Maryland Medical Center is a hospital in the Baltimore area, as well as a site that conducts clinical research.

66**Patients with photosensitive epilepsy may have seizures or unusual feelings that are triggered by flashing or flickering of lights, and rapidly changing patterns or images (such as television or video).**99

—Jacqueline French, "A Photosensitivity Study," Epilepsy Therapy Project, January 4, 2008. www.epilepsy.com.

French is the director of the Clinical Trials Consortium at New York University's Comprehensive Epilepsy Center.

* Editor's Note: While the definition of a primary source can be narrowly or broadly defined, for the purposes of Compact Research, a primary source consists of: 1) results of original research presented by an organization or researcher; 2) eyewitness accounts of events, personal experience, or work experience; 3) first-person editorials offering pundits' opinions; 4) government officials presenting political plans and/or policies; 5) representatives of organizations presenting testimony or policy.

> **For most individuals, a first seizure can be a dramatic event and it is certainly something [for which] people would seek medical attention.**

—David Clarke, "If I Had Uncontrolled Epilepsy," Insider Medicine, December 22, 2008. www.insidermedicine.com.

Clarke is an associate professor in the Department of Surgery, Division of Neurosurgery and Neurobiology, at Dalhousie University in Nova Scotia, Canada.

> **At first we went into denial: Lydia seemed so perfect—not only was she hitting her milestones on time or early, but she glowed with good health, was energetic and happy. Then the seizures began increasing in frequency and we went into a panic.**

—Camilla Beckett, interviewed by Rita Watson, "Childhood Epilepsy: What You Need to Know," Epilepsy Therapy Project, March 28, 2008. www.epilepsy.com.

Beckett, the mother of a 10-year-old girl with epilepsy, is a professional filmmaker who produces educational films about the disorder.

> **A person having a severe seizure may cry out, fall to the floor unconscious, twitch or move uncontrollably, drool, or even lose bladder control.**

—National Institute of Neurological Disorders and Stroke, "Seizures and Epilepsy: Hope Through Research," April 24, 2009. www.ninds.nih.gov.

The mission of the National Institute of Neurological Disorders and Stroke is to reduce the burden of neurological disease.

> **I would wake up abruptly with a huge adrenaline rush, next a sense of foreboding, and then my body would start to convulse. It was incredibly painful and I would try to shout for help.**

—Susan Brown, "Gain Control of Your Seizures," *Epilepsy: Insights and Strategies*, April 2009. www.epilepsy.com.

Brown, who has epilepsy, works with students who have disabilities.

"There is a stigma. People are afraid and even the most educated do not understand epilepsy and seizures."

—Debra Josephs, interviewed by Rita Watson, "Teaching People About Seizures," Epilepsy Therapy Project, May 1, 2008. www.epilepsy.com.

Josephs is executive director of the Anita Kaufman Foundation, which is dedicated to raising public awareness about epilepsy.

"It was because of acting that I recognized that my seizures could be triggered by light. Unfortunately, I did not make this connection until I had a seizure on stage."

—Ann Carletta, "Choosing Epilepsy Surgery," *Epilepsy: Insights and Strategies*, April 2009. www.epilepsy.com.

Carletta is a woman with epilepsy who had seizures for 36 years before having surgery and who is now seizure free.

Facts and Illustrations

What Is Epilepsy?

- According to the World Health Organization, epilepsy affects an estimated **50 million** people throughout the world, with about **90 percent** living in developing countries.

- Between **2.5 million** and **3 million** people in the United States have epilepsy.

- According to the National Institute of Neurological Disorders and Stroke, currently available treatments can control seizures at least some of the time in **80 percent** of people with epilepsy.

- Neurologist Martha Morrell states that although **1 in every 10** persons has a seizure in his or her lifetime, only **1 out of 100** develop epilepsy.

- There are more than **20** different types of seizures, which are broadly classified into two groups: primary generalized seizures and partial seizure groups.

- According to the University of Maryland Medical Center, about **10 percent** of Americans will experience at least one seizure during their lifetime.

- The Epilepsy Foundation states that **326,000** American schoolchildren through age 15 have epilepsy.

Epileptic Seizures and the Brain

Scientists have identified numerous types of seizures and typically categorize them in two different groups: focal seizures and generalized seizures. Focal seizures (also called partial seizures) originate in just one part of the brain, most commonly the frontal lobe, whereas generalized seizures originate in any part of the brain and are typically much more severe. This illustration shows where the four lobes are located in the brain and what their functions are.

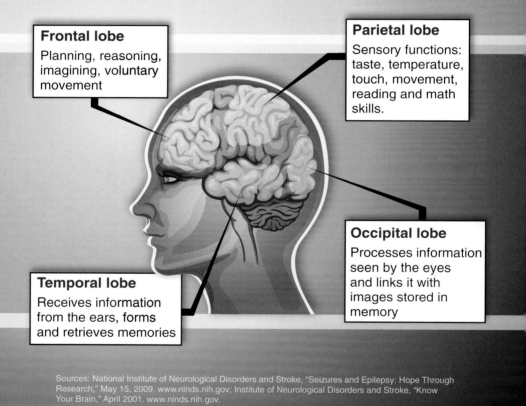

Frontal lobe
Planning, reasoning, imagining, voluntary movement

Parietal lobe
Sensory functions: taste, temperature, touch, movement, reading and math skills.

Occipital lobe
Processes information seen by the eyes and links it with images stored in memory

Temporal lobe
Receives information from the ears, forms and retrieves memories

Sources: National Institute of Neurological Disorders and Stroke, "Seizures and Epilepsy: Hope Through Research," May 15, 2009. www.ninds.nih.gov; Institute of Neurological Disorders and Stroke, "Know Your Brain," April 2001. www.ninds.nih.gov.

- An estimated **14 percent** of epilepsy patients are under 15 years old, and about **25 percent** are over 64.

A Common Neurological Disorder

According to the Epilepsy Foundation nearly 3 million people in the United States suffer from epilepsy. The only neurological disorders that are more common than epilepsy are stroke and Alzheimer's disease.

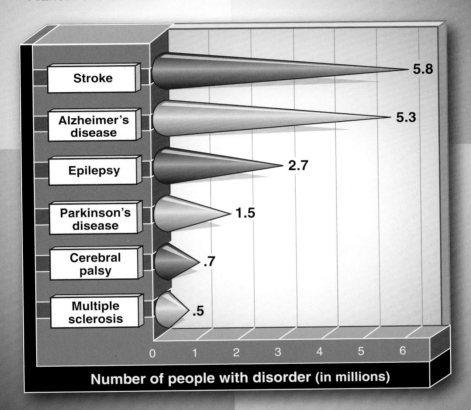

Number of people with disorder (in millions)

Sources: Epilepsy Foundation, "Epilepsy: Just the Facts," March 4, 2008. www.epilepsyfoundation.org; Alzheimer's Association, "2009 Alzheimer's Disease Facts and Figures," February 12, 2009. www.alz.org; American Heart Association and American Stroke Association, "Heart Disease and Stroke Statistics," 2008. www.americanheart.org.

- The Centers for Disease Control and Prevention states that about **200,000** new cases of epilepsy are diagnosed each year in the United States.

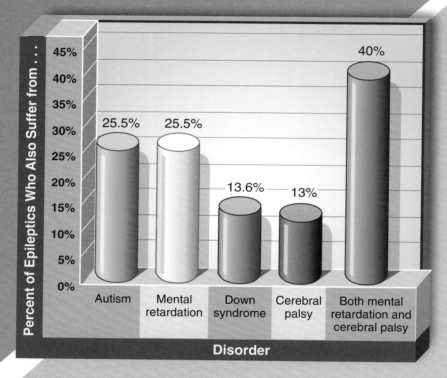

Coexisting Conditions

Those who suffer from epilepsy often have other physical and/or mental disabilities, as this graph illustrates. Forty percent of those with epilepsy also suffer from both mental retardation and cerebral palsy.

Source: Epilepsy Foundation, "Epilepsy: Just the Facts," March 4, 2008. www.epilepsyfoundation.org.

- In a poll published in January 2008 by the Epilepsy Therapy Project, **88 percent** of respondents (all of whom have epilepsy) said that it is harder for people with epilepsy to obtain health insurance in the United States.

- The Epilepsy Foundation states that **3 percent** of Americans will develop epilepsy by the age of 75.

Impaired Quality of Life

Studies have shown that people with epilepsy often suffer from health-related issues that have a negative impact on their quality of life. This graph illustrates how participants in a survey by the Centers for Disease Control and Prevention responded when asked about some of these issues.

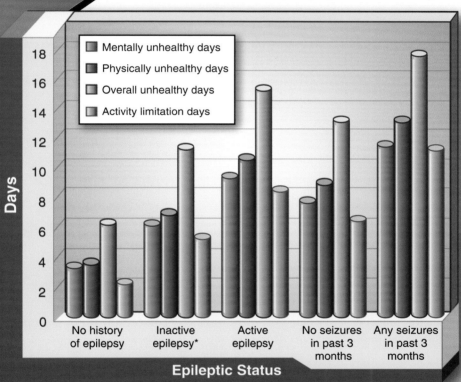

Health-Related Quality of Life for Adults with and Without Epilepsy—Past 30 Days

*Respondents diagnosed with epilepsy, but who had not had a seizure in the past 3 months and were not taking medications

Source: Centers for Disease Control and Prevention, "Targeting Epilepsy," 2009. www.cdc.gov.

- According to the advocacy group People Against Childhood Epilepsy, an estimated **20** to **30 percent** of people with epilepsy who are physically able to work are unemployed.

What Causes Epilepsy?

66Epilepsy is a disorder with many possible causes. Anything that disturbs the normal pattern of neuron activity—from illness to brain damage to abnormal brain development—can lead to seizures.99

—National Institute of Neurological Disorders and Stroke, whose mission is to reduce the burden of neurological disease.

66The seizures in epilepsy may be related to a brain injury or a family tendency, but most of the time the cause is unknown.99

—Carol Camfield, professor of pediatrics at the Dalhousie University Medical School in Nova Scotia, Canada, and Robert S. Fisher, neurology professor and director of the Stanford Comprehensive Epilepsy Center.

One of the most frustrating things for those who have epilepsy, as well as for their families, is being told "we do not know" when they ask what caused it. Unfortunately, though, that answer is not at all uncommon. According to the Epilepsy Foundation, no cause can be found in about 7 out of 10 people who have the disorder. One epilepsy sufferer to whom this applies is Lauren Axelrod, a young woman from Chicago who started having seizures when she was a baby. Lauren seemed to be perfectly healthy and was developing normally until she was seven months old. One evening her mother, Susan Axelrod, gave her a small dose of medication to help relieve cold symptoms, and then tucked her into bed for the night. The next morning she went into Lauren's room and was terrified to find the baby limp in her crib. "I thought she was dead," says Axelrod. "In shock, I picked her up, and she went into a seizure—arms extended, eyes rolling back in her head. I realized she'd most likely been having seizures all night long. I phoned my mother and cried, 'This is normal, right? Babies do this?' She said, 'No, they don't.'"[26]

Lauren was diagnosed with idiopathic epilepsy, meaning of unknown origin, and at times had as many as 25 seizures per day. By the time she was a teenager she had suffered mental impairment, and her seizures were growing more severe. "I thought we were about to lose her," says Axelrod. "Her doctor said, 'I don't know what else we can do.'"[27] Fortunately, a new anticonvulsant drug became available, and as soon as Lauren started taking it, her seizures stopped.

The Genetic Link

Although no cause has ever been determined for idiopathic epilepsy, scientists believe that it has genetic ties. According to neurologists Elizabeth Donner and Berge Minassian, research has shown that if a parent has idiopathic epilepsy, there is a 9 to 12 percent chance that the child will also have it. They say that even though hereditary forms of epilepsy are uncommon, if a child has epilepsy, his or her siblings have a higher risk of developing it. Also, if one twin has epilepsy, his or her identical twin is highly likely to have it as well. Donner and Minassian emphasize the importance of genetics in the development of various types of epilepsy, as they explain: "Family studies have shown that some epilepsy syndromes are completely determined by genetics, and genes are a major factor in other syndromes." They add that the inheritance of epilepsy is often complex: "Two children with mutations on different genes may develop the same epilepsy syndrome. Two members of the same family with the same gene mutation may both develop epilepsy, but the effects in each person may be very different. Some epilepsy syndromes are known to have a genetic basis, but the specific gene or genes that cause them have not been identified."[28]

> One of the most frustrating things for those who have epilepsy, as well as for their families, is being told 'we do not know' when they ask what caused it.

Donner and Minassian point to at least 20 epilepsy syndromes that have been linked to specific genes. One example, which is caused by several possible gene mutations, is known as benign familial neonatal convulsions. The disorder usually appears several days after a baby is born and often causes severe seizures, although they typically last no more than a few weeks or a month. But, an estimated 11 to 16 percent of those who suffer from this type of epilepsy as babies experience seizures again, either during late childhood or, more commonly, when they are adults.

Another example of genetic-based epilepsy is Unverricht-Lundborg disease. The Epilepsy Therapy Project states that when a child inherits the disorder, his or her parents are both carriers of an abnormal gene. Known as cystatin B, the role of the gene is to protect neurons against enzymes that destroy essential proteins. The gene is located on chromosome 21, which is 1 of the 22 pairs of chromosomes in all the cells of the body. Unverricht-Lundborg symptoms usually appear between the ages of 6 and 18 and typically involve seizures that range from muscle twitching to full-blown tonic-clonic seizures. These are triggered in various ways, from periodic flashes of light, certain types of music or other noise, and/or stress.

> " According to neurologists Elizabeth Donner and Berge Minassian, research has shown that if a parent has idiopathic epilepsy, there is a 9 to 12 percent chance that the child will also have it. "

The prognosis for people who have this disorder is not as bleak as for some other types of epilepsy, but it does cause deterioration over time, as the Epilepsy Therapy Project states: "Unverricht-Lundborg has a slow progressive worsening of symptoms, both in seizure control and neurological functioning. The disease progresses slowly, with patients maintaining normal cognitive functioning for a long time and decline in intelligence being very slow. Moderate deterioration may take from 10 to 20 years. Most patients live 50–60 years before dying."[29]

A Vulnerable Organ: The Brain

Many types of epilepsy are either known or believed to have hereditary links, but epilepsy can also be caused by nongenetic factors. Anything that creates a disruption in normal brain activity can potentially result in someones developing epilepsy. For instance, if an individual suffers a stroke, there is a blockage of blood supply to certain parts of the brain, and this deprives the brain of oxygen. As the brain attempts to repair itself, scar tissue forms and becomes a foreign body to neurons, which can lead to abnormal electrical discharges. According to Columbia University physician and stroke specialist José Vega, epilepsy occurs in only about 2 to 4 percent of stroke survivors. He adds, however, that the risk grows as people age, as he explains: "Stroke is the most commonly identified cause of epilepsy in adults older than 35 and accounts for more than 50% of all new cases of epilepsy of known cause in the elderly population."[30]

> " **Anything that creates a disruption in normal brain activity can potentially result in someones developing epilepsy.** "

In addition to stroke, benign or malignant brain tumors can lead to epilepsy. Research has shown that more than one-third of those who are newly diagnosed with brain tumors develop epileptic seizures sometime during their lives. If the tumor involves the cerebral hemispheres, the largest area of the brain, the risk of developing epilepsy increases to about 50 percent. An extremely rare type known as gelastic epilepsy is usually caused by a small brain tumor. The word *gelastic* is derived from the Greek word *gelastikos*, meaning "laughter," and it is a fitting name for the disorder because those who have it often start laughing before the onset of seizures. Pediatric neurologist Richard Appleton explains: "The laughter is often described as being 'hollow' or 'empty' and not very pleasant. The laughter occurs suddenly, comes on for no obvious reason and is usually completely out of place."[31] Appleton adds that seizures may begin at any age, but commonly start when a child is three or four years old.

Because severe head injuries often cause brain damage, they can lead to the development of epilepsy. When Anita Kaufmann was 14 years old, she was thrown from a horse while riding at summer camp. She was not wearing protective headgear and sustained a head injury as a result of her fall. After spending 4 days in a coma and several months in the hospital, Kaufmann seemed to be fully recovered. She achieved excellent grades in high school and went on to the University of Pennsylvania, where she graduated with honors, and then earned her law degree from Georgetown University. She became very successful and her career was blossoming—but when she was in her thirties, she had her first seizure while vacationing at a spa. The diagnosis was epilepsy, brought on by the head injury she had sustained nearly 20 years before. On November 26, 2003, Kaufmann died at the age of 49 as a result of complications from a seizure.

> " Military personnel who serve in war zones have an extremely high potential for suffering severe head injuries and are therefore prone to developing epilepsy. "

Military personnel who serve in war zones have an extremely high potential for suffering severe head injuries and are therefore prone to developing epilepsy. An expert on this topic is John Booss, who is a veteran of the U.S. Air Force and the former national director of neurology at the Department of Veterans Affairs (VA). Booss states that individuals who sustain traumatic brain injury may develop post-traumatic seizures months or even years after the injury occurred. Although data are not available for post-traumatic epilepsy among those who have served in Afghanistan or Iraq, Booss points to statistics from the Vietnam War, which he calls "alarming." Research that was cofunded by the VA and the U.S. Department of Defense showed that 53 percent of veterans who suffered a penetrating brain injury during the conflict developed epilepsy within 15 years. "For these service-connected veterans," he states, "the relative risk for developing epilepsy more than 10 to 15 years after their injury was 25 times higher than their age-related civilian cohorts. Indeed, 15 percent did not manifest epilepsy until five or more years after their combat injury."[32]

Preventable Epilepsy

The development of some types of epilepsy in children has been linked to unhealthy lifestyles by pregnant women, such as poor nutrition, lack of prenatal care, smoking, and taking drugs. One of the most serious risks to the unborn child is fetal alcohol syndrome (FAS), which is a direct result of women drinking alcohol while they are pregnant. The alcohol has a much greater impact on the fetus than on the mother, as genetics counselor Linda Nicholson explains: "Because alcohol easily passes the placental barrier and the fetus is less equipped to eliminate alcohol than its mother, the fetus tends to receive a high concentration of alcohol, which lingers longer than it would in the mother's system."[33] FAS can cause serious damage to a fetus's central nervous system, and babies who are born with it may suffer from a variety of physical and mental disabilities. These include mental retardation, vision and hearing problems, developmental delays, learning disabilities, and disorders such as epilepsy.

One type of epilepsy that has been linked to both genetics and environmental factors such as alcohol use by pregnant women is known as juvenile myoclonic epilepsy (JME). It is one of the most common types, with symptoms usually becoming apparent between the ages of 12 and 16. People who suffer from JME typically have myoclonic seizures, which involve quick little jerks of the arms, shoulders, and/or legs and usually occur in the morning soon after the person wakes up. These seizures may be triggered by flickering lights, television, video games, or light that reflects off ocean waves or snow. According to the Epilepsy Therapy Project, myoclonic seizures can also be triggered by mental processes such as decision making or calculations, and they are often followed by severe tonic-clonic seizures.

> " Since epilepsy occurs as a result of abnormal neuronal activity, the disorder can result from certain types of infectious disease that affect the brain. "

The Infection Connection

Since epilepsy occurs as a result of abnormal neuronal activity, the disorder can result from certain types of infectious diseases that affect the brain. For instance, epilepsy has been linked to meningitis, which is an infection of the membrane around the spinal cord and brain. Epilepsy may also result from encephalitis, an acute inflammation of the brain that is usually caused by a bacterial or viral infection. This happened to Stacey

Chillemi, who developed encephalitis when she was 5 years old after having an ear infection. For 4 days Chillemi was in a coma, and doctors did not know the extent of her brain damage, nor did they know whether she would be paralyzed for life. She recovered from the encephalitis but later developed epilepsy. Since she was diagnosed 27 years ago, Chillemi has had seizures ranging in severity from mild episodes that occur during her sleep to full-blown tonic-clonic seizures.

Another disease that can lead to epilepsy is neurocysticercosis (NCC), which is a parasitic infection of the nervous system. NCC results from eating food that is contaminated by the *Taenia solium* tapeworm, and it usually originates in undercooked pork products. According to the Epilepsy Society, NCC is the most common of all parasitic diseases and the leading cause of epilepsy in developing countries, especially Latin America, India, Africa, and China.

Complex Causes

Decades of research have allowed scientists to pinpoint the cause of numerous diseases, from influenza and AIDS to diabetes and leukemia. But epilepsy is nothing like those diseases and, in fact, is not a disease at all. Epilepsy comprises a number of highly complex disorders that stem from factors such as genetics, environment, and physical ailments like brain injury and infections. Although researchers have made excellent progress in identifying a number of contributors to the onset of epilepsy, much about its causes remains mysterious. As research continues in the future, the myriad complexities of this disorder may finally be resolved.

Primary Source Quotes*

What Causes Epilepsy?

66Epilepsy has many possible causes, including illness, brain injury and abnormal brain development. In many cases, the cause is unknown.99

—National Institutes of Health, "Epilepsy," Medline Plus, May 12, 2009. www.nlm.nih.gov.

The National Institutes of Health is the United States' primary agency for conducting and supporting medical research.

66Science is unraveling more and more of the mysteries of the brain, and perhaps the source of the cataclysmic electrical storms of epilepsy will yield its secrets.99

—Jon Meacham, "A Storm in the Brain," *Newsweek*, April 11, 2009. www.newsweek.com.

Meacham is the editor of *Newsweek* magazine.

* Editor's Note: While the definition of a primary source can be narrowly or broadly defined, for the purposes of Compact Research, a primary source consists of: 1) results of original research presented by an organization or researcher; 2) eyewitness accounts of events, personal experience, or work experience; 3) first-person editorials offering pundits' opinions; 4) government officials presenting political plans and/or policies; 5) representatives of organizations presenting testimony or policy.

Primary Source Quotes

❝There are many kinds of seizures, but all involve abnormal electrical activity in the brain that causes an involuntary change in body movement or function, sensation, awareness, or behavior.❞

—Centers for Disease Control and Prevention, "Epilepsy," April 1, 2008. www.cdc.gov.

The Centers for Disease Control and Prevention is a federal agency charged with promoting health and quality of life by controlling disease, injury, and disability.

❝High fevers in childhood can sometimes be associated with prolonged seizures and subsequent epilepsy later in life, particularly for those with a family history of epilepsy.❞

—Mayo Clinic, "Epilepsy: Causes," July 1, 2008. www.mayoclinic.com.

The Mayo Clinic is a medical practice that is dedicated to the diagnosis and treatment of virtually every type of complex illness.

❝At a chemical signal, whose origin is still a mystery, billions of neurons drop the mundane business of running the body and join in a primitive drumbeat, drowning out the murmur of consciousness.❞

—Jerry Adler and Eliza Gray, "In the Grip of the Unknown," *Newsweek*, April 11, 2009. www.newsweek.com.

Adler is senior editor, and Gray a contributing writer, of *Newsweek* magazine.

❝The cause depends on the age of onset. Severe epilepsy early in life is often associated with developmental abnormalities or birth injury.❞

—*GP*, "Clinical: Review—Epilepsy," October 31, 2008.

GP is a publication for general practitioners in the United Kingdom.

66Lack of knowledge about the causes of epilepsy has been associated with negative attitudes, beliefs, and stigma.99

—Centers for Disease Control and Prevention, *Targeting Epilepsy*, 2009. www.cdc.gov.

The Centers for Disease Control and Prevention is a federal agency charged with promoting health and quality of life by controlling disease, injury, and disability.

66Most cases of epilepsy are not inherited, although some types are genetically transmitted (that is, passed on through the family).99

—Orrin Devinsky, "Facts & Myths," Epilepsy Therapy Project, November 13, 2008. www.epilepsy.com.

Devinsky is the director of the New York University Comprehensive Epilepsy Center.

66The risk of epilepsy shortly after traumatic brain injury is high, but how long this high risk lasts is unknown.99

—J. Christensen et al., "Long-Term Risk of Epilepsy After Traumatic Brain Injury in Children and Young Adults," *Lancet*, March 2009. www.ncbi.nlm.nih.gov.

Christensen is with the Department of Neurology at Aarhus University Hospital in Aarhus, Denmark.

What Causes Epilepsy?

- According to the group People Against Childhood Epilepsy (PACE), in about **75 percent** of epilepsy cases there is no known cause.

- Cedars-Sinai Medical Center states that children are more likely than adults to develop epilepsy from an unknown cause.

- The Mayo Clinic states that researchers have linked some types of epilepsy to specific genes, but as many as **500 genes** could be tied to the condition.

- According to the Epilepsy Foundation, some studies have shown that the risk of epilepsy in brothers, sisters, and children of people with the disorder ranges from **4 to 8 percent**, compared to **1 to 2 percent** in the general population.

- According to the Mayo Clinic, stroke is responsible for up to one-half of epilepsy cases in people older than age 65.

- About **20 percent** of seizures in children are associated with cerebral palsy or other neurological disorders.

- Health officials state that between **25 and 50 percent** of people who suffer a severe brain injury will eventually develop epilepsy.

A Complex Disorder

Because there are numerous types of epilepsy (often referred to as "epilepsies" or "epilepsy syndromes") no one cause can be identified. Scientists believe that there are numerous contributing factors.

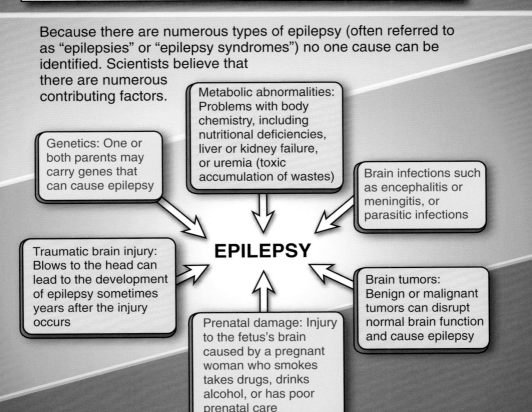

Metabolic abnormalities: Problems with body chemistry, including nutritional deficiencies, liver or kidney failure, or uremia (toxic accumulation of wastes)

Genetics: One or both parents may carry genes that can cause epilepsy

Brain infections such as encephalitis or meningitis, or parasitic infections

Traumatic brain injury: Blows to the head can lead to the development of epilepsy sometimes years after the injury occurs

EPILEPSY

Brain tumors: Benign or malignant tumors can disrupt normal brain function and cause epilepsy

Prenatal damage: Injury to the fetus's brain caused by a pregnant woman who smokes takes drugs, drinks alcohol, or has poor prenatal care

Source: U.S. National Library of Medicine and the National Institutes of Health, "Medical Encyclopedia: Epilepsy," May 4, 2009. www.nlm.nih.gov.

- Post-traumatic epilepsy (caused by traumatic brain injury) is thought to be responsible for about **20 percent** of seizures in people with the disorder.

- The Epilepsy Foundation states only a few rare types of epilepsy are caused by **alterations in single genes**, and most seem to be caused by a complex interaction among multiple genes and environmental influences.

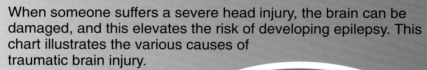

The Most Common Causes of Traumatic Brain Injury (TBI)

When someone suffers a severe head injury, the brain can be damaged, and this elevates the risk of developing epilepsy. This chart illustrates the various causes of traumatic brain injury.

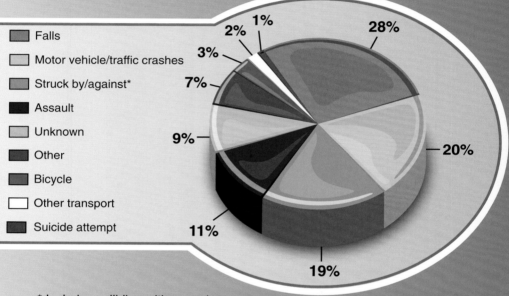

- Falls
- Motor vehicle/traffic crashes
- Struck by/against*
- Assault
- Unknown
- Other
- Bicycle
- Other transport
- Suicide attempt

1%
2%
3%
7%
9%
11%
19%
20%
28%

* Includes colliding with a moving or stationary object, often sports- and recreation-related TBIs.

Source: Centers for Disease Control and Prevention, "What Is Traumatic Brain Injury?" September 21, 2007. www.cdc.gov.

- According to the National Institute of Neurological Disorders and Stroke, factors that influence a child's risk of having **recurrent febrile seizures** (seizures caused by high fever) include young age (less than 15 months), frequent fevers, and having immediate family members with a history of febrile seizures.

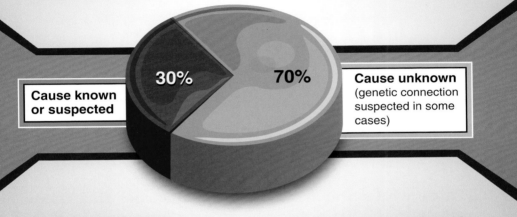

Majority of Epilepsy Cases Do Not Have a Known Cause

Although much about epilepsy's causes remains mysterious to scientists, research has shown that there are a number of contributing factors—but for the majority of epilepsy sufferers, no cause can be determined.

30%

70%

Cause known or suspected

Cause unknown (genetic connection suspected in some cases)

Source: National Institute of Neurological Disorders and Stroke, "Curing Epilepsy: The Promise of Research," April 24, 2009. www.ninds.nih.gov.

- In October 2007 researchers from the Howard Florey Institute in Melbourne, Australia, discovered that a **mutation** in a single gene can cause epilepsy in infants.

- The Epilepsy Therapy Project states that the general population has about a **1 percent** risk of developing epilepsy, while children of mothers with epilepsy have a **3 to 9 percent** risk, and children of fathers with epilepsy have a **1.5 to 3 percent** risk.

What Are the Risks Associated with Epilepsy?

66Epilepsy more than doubles the risk of dying.99

—Robert S. Fisher, neurology professor and director of the Stanford Epilepsy Center.

66Those who suffer from the brain disorder find themselves in the grip of forces—forces from within their own bodies, their own beings—that they cannot control. It is terrifying. And it can be deadly.99

—Jon Meacham, editor of *Newsweek* magazine.

By the time Richard Gray was 64 years old, he had been having seizures for nearly his entire life, and this left him unable to drive or work at a job to support his family. In July 2008 he entered a Colorado hospital for tests so that doctors could learn more about what was causing the seizures and determine whether he was a potential candidate for surgery. The medication that Gray regularly took to control his epilepsy was stopped in order to induce a seizure intentionally, which was the only way doctors could determine where the epilepsy originated in his brain. Upon being admitted to the hospital, Gray was assured that he would be monitored around the clock because a seizure could happen at any time—but on the fourth night of his stay he was left alone for an hour. A videotape in his room captured him having a seizure, during which he pressed his face into the pillow, cutting off his oxygen supply and causing him to stop breathing. Another 30 minutes passed before a technologist returned to Gray's room and found him dead. According to Steven Ringel, a physician at the hospital, if someone had been monitoring Gray at the time of his death, it is very likely that he would have survived.

Death for No Apparent Reason

Seizures are not usually deadly, but they can potentially cause brain damage, as Duke University neurologist Mohamad Mikati explains: "If seizures are not controlled, especially if they are frequent and violent, they can injure the brain."[34] In general, people who suffer from epilepsy have a higher risk of dying compared to those who do not have the disorder. One of the most puzzling, as well as frightening, occurrences is known as sudden unexpected death in epilepsy (SUDEP). Although it is extremely rare, scientists say that SUDEP claims the lives of as many as 17 percent of those who have epilepsy, yet why this occurs is not known. According to the group Epilepsy Action, research has suggested that the part of the brain that controls breathing may be affected by epilepsy, which could cause the person to stop breathing during a major seizure. Most people would start breathing again once the seizure ends, but for unknown reasons that does not happen in people who die from SUDEP.

In November 2008 a team of neurologists from the University of California–Davis Medical Center published a SUDEP study that appeared to confirm Epilepsy Action's theory. The researchers examined medical records of people who had died from SUDEP, as well as the records of 57 epilepsy patients with chronic, recurrent seizures. After comparing patients with severe convulsive seizures to those with milder symptoms such as confusion, lip smacking, and head turning, the researchers determined that some cases of SUDEP may result from the brain not signaling the person to continue breathing during seizures. Senior author Masud Seyal explains: "It may have to do with an abnormal heart rhythm or it just may be that the brain stops sending the proper signals to maintain normal breathing."[35] Seyal and fellow researchers found that the sei-

> " Seizures are not usually deadly, but they can potentially cause brain damage. "

zures of one-third of those examined were associated with sharp drops in blood-oxygen levels. This is an important finding because it shows a likely connection between blood-oxygen levels and seizures, which may explain why people who die from SUDEP suddenly quit breathing.

> **If the seizures associated with status epilepticus do not respond to drug treatments (a condition known as refractory status epilepticus), this presents a dangerous situation.**

In April 2009 a woman named Marlene McElligott posted on the Epilepsy Action Web site about her 14-year-old son who died from SUDEP. He had developed epilepsy in 2005 after being stricken with encephalitis and immediately began to have seizures. When an EEG came back normal in June 2008, McElligott began weaning her son off antiepileptic drugs on the advice of his physician. "The doctors told us that if anything was going to happen it would happen while he was weaning off the medication and believe me SUDEP was not ever mentioned," she writes. "Why isn't this told to parents?!"[36] Six months later the boy was dead. McElligott found him in bed one morning with his dog still sleeping next to him. Tests later showed that his heart had stopped due to a lack of oxygen from a seizure that he had likely had during the night.

A Life-Threatening Condition

Much more common than SUDEP is status epilepticus (SE), a neurological disorder that can be deadly if it is not caught and treated immediately. Neurologist Mark Spitz describes SE as an "acute, prolonged epileptic crisis,"[37] and says that it involves someone having a seizure that lasts for more than 30 minutes or experiencing 2 or more seizures between which the person does not regain full consciousness. Spitz adds that up to 70 percent of SE cases occur in children, but the risk is also high in adults who are 60 years of age or older. The most common cause of SE is a change in medication, either directed by a physician or due to intentional or unintentional cessation by the patient. The risks posed by SE include irreversible brain damage, physical injuries due to falling, and death.

If the seizures associated with status epilepticus do not respond to drug treatments (a condition known as refractory status epilepticus), this presents a dangerous situation. The only way to save a patient may be to put him or her in a temporary coma so the seizures will stop. Neurologist Andrea Rossetti explains: "In the case of refractory status epilepticus, the seizure has no stopping mechanism. Unlike other types of seizures, which eventually stop on their own, these seizures do not stop and require drastic medical intervention, such as coma induction, to allow the brain to rest. By inducing a coma, we make it less likely that seizures will recur, at least during the period of intense treatment."[38] One of Orrin Devinsky's epilepsy patients, a teenage boy, went to a hospital emergency room with SE in December 2008. When Devinsky could not stop the seizures, he induced a coma, and the boy has remained in one ever since. In the meantime Devinsky is looking for the right combination of drugs that will get the boy's seizures under control and hopefully save his life.

Preventable Deaths

The very fact that an epilepsy sufferer may suddenly have a seizure is a risk. For instance, if someone has a seizure while driving a vehicle, the result could be a deadly crash. This occurred in March 2009 in Seminole, Florida, when 19-year-old Kyle Figler suffered a violent seizure as he was driving near a mall. His car left the road and veered onto a sidewalk, where it slammed into 2 people who were walking. One of the pedestrians was killed instantly, and the other was seriously injured. Figler was not hurt in the crash.

In another case that occurred in May 2008, a woman from Lindbergh, Missouri, had a seizure while driving, ran off the roadway, and struck a glass-enclosed bus stop. Police officers said that the force of the crash pushed the bus stop off its foundation and into the roadway, where it struck a vehicle. Two teenagers had been inside the structure waiting for the bus, and one of them, 17-year-old Elijah Moore, was critically

> **[Researchers] learned that compared to those in the general population, people with epilepsy had 15 to 19 times the risk of drowning.**

injured and died shortly thereafter. The driver and her passenger only sustained minor injuries.

Another potentially dangerous situation for those who have epilepsy is the risk of drowning, which was the subject of a study published in the August 19, 2008, issue of *Neurology*. Researchers examined worldwide records of people with epilepsy, as well as population data and national registries, to determine how many drowning deaths occur and the likely causes. They learned that compared to those in the general population, people with epilepsy had 15 to 19 times the risk of drowning. "It is important that people with epilepsy and their caregivers take steps to prevent these tragedies," says study author Ley Sander, who is with the Institute of Neurology at University College-London in the United Kingdom. "People with active epilepsy should shower instead of bathe, take medication regularly to control seizures and should have direct supervision when swimming."[39]

> **He had a seizure, fell face-first into the fire, and suffered severe third- and fourth-degree burns to his nose, eyes, eyelids, and forehead, as well as to both arms and hands.**

A tragic example of a seizure-related drowning death occurred in December 2005. Michael Meyers, a 36-year-old man from Carlsbad, California, suffered a seizure while surfing off a Carlsbad beach. Meyers, who was an experienced surfer, had developed epilepsy after suffering a severe head injury 10 years before. At the time of his seizure, he was sitting on his surfboard and lost consciousness, fell into the water, and drowned.

Severe Burn Injuries

For those who have epilepsy, even performing simple tasks such as cooking or building a campfire can be dangerous because if they have a seizure, they can be badly burned. This happened to Christopher Mance when he was attending Ohio University and went on a wilderness survival trip during Memorial Day weekend in 2006. Mance took medication to control his seizures, but it was less effective during the camping trip because his normal sleeping and eating patterns were disrupted. While alone in a secluded area of the forest, he was stoking a campfire per the instructor's requirement that he maintain it all night. He had a seizure, fell face-first into the fire, and suffered severe third- and fourth-degree burns to his nose, eyes, eyelids, and forehead, as well as to both arms and hands. The burns also damaged the frontal lobe and other areas of his brain. Mance was not discovered until early the next morning, when another student heard him calling for help. The student and an instructor found Mance sitting against a tree and were shocked by how badly disfigured he was.

Risks During Pregnancy

Pregnant women who have epilepsy and take antiepileptic drugs are usually advised to continue taking them during pregnancy. Neurologist C. Akos Szabo explains: "Epileptic seizures are potentially dangerous to the pregnant woman and the fetus. Isolated seizures can lead to falls or other forms of physical injury, while frequent or prolonged seizures can lead to physical stress endangering the health of the woman and fetus." Szabo adds, however, that these medications present a potential risk to the fetus. Certain drugs have been linked to congenital malformations in the fetus's brain, spinal cord, heart, kidneys, genitals, and skeleton, as well as fetal death. He refers to one study that examined outcomes of 333 pregnancies in women for whom drugs kept seizures under control. The rate of all serious adverse effects to fetuses was 9 percent, which is more than twice as high as the general population. Of those, congenital malformations occurred in 7 percent of the cases. "In summary," writes Szabo, "there is mounting evidence that the risk for

> " A study published in December 2008 found that pregnant women who take the epilepsy drug sodium valproate may increase their babies' risk of developing autism. "

fetal death and congenital malformations in mothers with epilepsy may be affected by the medication they are prescribed. . . . Physicians and women of childbearing age both need to be aware of these risks when choosing the appropriate seizure medication during pregnancy."[40]

A study published in December 2008 found that pregnant women who take the epilepsy drug sodium valproate may increase their babies' risk of developing autism, which is a complex disorder that affects the brain's normal development. Researchers from the United Kingdom concluded that babies who were exposed to the drug while in the womb were seven times more likely to develop autism than those who had not been exposed to any epilepsy drugs. Yet as disturbing as this finding is, most physicians say that women have a greater risk of harming the fetus if they do not take their medications. Michael Goldstein, who is vice present of the American Academy of Neurology, explains: "Prolonged seizure could cause blood flow problems to the baby, which could cause injury." Goldstein adds that physicians generally try to avoid giving sodium valproate to women who might be pregnant, although in some cases no other drugs help control seizures. "They're better off taking the medicine than having seizures," he says. "The consensus is that seizures are worse for the babies than the medicine."[41]

"It's Kind of Heartbreaking"

Numerous people who suffer from epilepsy lead normal, healthy lives, but those whose seizures are not under control face a number of risks. If they have seizures while driving, they can injure or kill themselves as well as others. They risk drowning if they swim alone and severe burns if they seize while near a stove or fire. Epilepsy sufferers are also at risk of dying suddenly for unknown reasons or developing life-threatening status epilepticus. Because seizures are a fact of life for many with epilepsy, this can cause frustration as well as depression. When Dan Wheeless's seizures started again after years of being seizure free, he expressed how he felt about that: "It's kind of heartbreaking. I would love to not have epilepsy."[42]

What Are the Risks Associated with Epilepsy?

66**There is an increased mortality rate in people with epilepsy from drowning, accidents . . . and suicide, as well as sudden unexpected death in epilepsy (SUDEP) in which no cause is found on autopsy.**99

—Sarah Goodman, "Epilepsy: Diagnosis and Management," *Practice Nurse*, January 11, 2008.

Goodman is with the faculty of nursing and midwifery at the University of Sydney in Sidney, Australia.

66**People with epilepsy have an increased risk of poor self-esteem, depression, and suicide.**99

—National Institute of Neurological Disorders and Stroke, "Seizures and Epilepsy: Hope Through Research," April 24, 2009. www.ninds.nih.gov.

The mission of the National Institute of Neurological Disorders and Stroke is to reduce the burden of neurological disease.

* Editor's Note: While the definition of a primary source can be narrowly or broadly defined, for the purposes of Compact Research, a primary source consists of: 1) results of original research presented by an organization or researcher; 2) eyewitness accounts of events, personal experience, or work experience; 3) first-person editorials offering pundits' opinions; 4) government officials presenting political plans and/or policies; 5) representatives of organizations presenting testimony or policy.

❝If you have epilepsy, you're more than 15 times more likely to drown while swimming or bathing than the rest of the population because of the possibility of having a seizure while in the water.❞

—Mayo Clinic, "Epilepsy: Complications," April 28, 2009. www.mayoclinic.com.

The Mayo Clinic is a medical practice that is dedicated to the diagnosis and treatment of virtually every type of complex illness.

❝Although the majority of children born to women with epilepsy are normal, they are at increased risk for malformations as well as for poor neuropsychological outcomes.❞

—Kimford J. Meador, "Effects of In Utero Antiepileptic Drug Exposure," *Epilepsy Currents*, November/December 2008. www.aesnet.org.

Meador is a neurology professor and the director of the University of Florida's epilepsy program.

❝Any type of seizure, no matter how slight or brief, can affect your ability to drive safely.❞

—Epilepsy Action, "Why You Should Stop Driving When You Have Had a Seizure," November 2008. www.epilepsy.org.uk.

Epilepsy Action is the largest member-led epilepsy organization in Great Britain.

❝Suicidal thoughts can occur following seizures and some medications have been found to be associated with the occurrence of suicidal thoughts.❞

—Andres M. Kanner, "A Chat on Moods and Seizure Medicines," Epilepsy Therapy Project, May 1, 2008. www.epilepsy.com.

Kanner is a professor of neurological sciences at Rush Medical College in Chicago.

"Sometimes epilepsy is a symptom of a more serious underlying condition such as a stroke or a tumor that carries an increased risk of death."

—Centers for Disease Control and Prevention, "Epilepsy: Frequently Asked Questions," March 20, 2009. www.cdc.gov.

The Centers for Disease Control and Prevention is a federal agency charged with promoting health and quality of life by controlling disease, injury, and disability.

"My absence seizures were very frightening; a bit like suddenly being drunk, with my mind not controlling my body properly. . . . It was alarming and disorienting to feel such a lack of control."

—Susan Brown, "Gain Control of Your Seizures," *Epilepsy: Insights and Strategies*, April 2009. www.epilepsy.com.

Brown, who has epilepsy, works with students who have disabilities.

What Are the Risks Associated with Epilepsy?

- The Mayo Clinic states that fewer than **1 in 1,000** people die from sudden unexplained death in epilepsy, but it is most common among people whose seizures are not controlled by treatment.

- According to the World Health Organization, a person with epilepsy is **2 to 3 times** more likely to die prematurely than someone who does not have epilepsy.

- Although most pregnant women with epilepsy have healthy babies, all medicines to treat the disorder carry some risk of **birth defects**.

- In December 2008 a study published in the medical journal *Neurology* stated that a pregnant woman who uses the antiseizure drug sodium valproate is **7 times** more likely to have a child with autism than women who do not take the drug.

- In an April 2007 poll among people with epilepsy, **55 percent** of respondents said they either had no plan in place to prevent injuries from seizures or no one had ever talked to them about the necessity of having such a plan.

- Because of the risk of seizure, most states and the District of Columbia will not issue a driver's license to someone with epilepsy unless the person has been **seizure free** for a specified period of time. Periods vary from a few months to several years.

Epilepsy and Injuries

During a March/April 2007 poll by the Epilepsy Therapy Project, participants were asked questions about epilepsy-related injuries, and these charts show how they responded.

"Have you (or your loved one) ever been hospitalized for an injury from a seizure?"

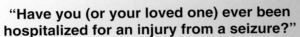
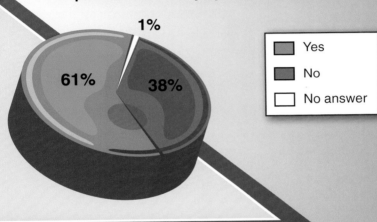

1%

61%

38%

- Yes
- No
- No answer

"What type of injuries have you (or your loved one) experienced as a result of a seizure?"

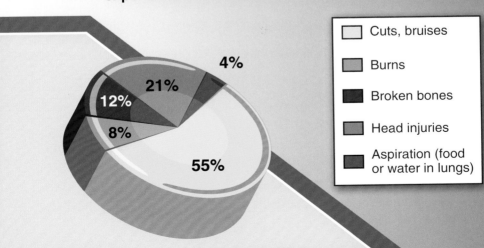

4%

21%

12%

8%

55%

- Cuts, bruises
- Burns
- Broken bones
- Head injuries
- Aspiration (food or water in lungs)

Source: Epilepsy Therapy Project, "Insta-Polls," July 2007. www.epilepsy.com.

Risk of Birth Defects to Fetus

Physicians recommend that women who have epilepsy continue taking their medications if they become pregnant because having seizures can be risky for them as well as for the fetus. But studies have shown that certain medications can cause fetal damage and even death. Children born to women taking antiepileptic medication have a 4 to 8 percent greater risk of birth defects than other children.

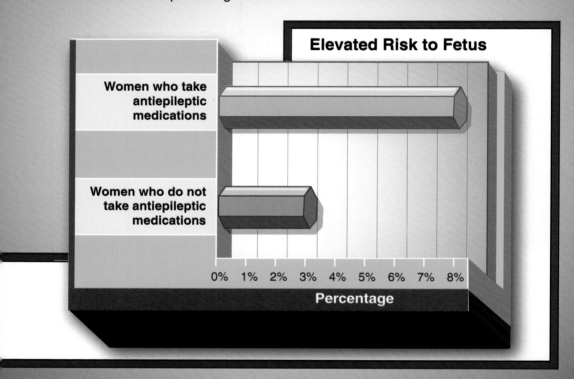

Elevated Risk to Fetus

Women who take antiepileptic medications

Women who do not take antiepileptic medications

0% 1% 2% 3% 4% 5% 6% 7% 8%

Percentage

Source: Mayo Clinic, "Epilepsy and Pregnancy: Healthy Choices for a Healthy Baby," April 1, 2007. www.mayoclinic.com.

- According to a study published in August 2008 by researchers from the Centers for Disease Control and Prevention's National Center for Chronic Disease Prevention and Health Promotion, adults with a history of epilepsy were more likely to be **obese, physically inactive, and current smokers.**

Epilepsy Drugs and Suicide

In January 2008 the U.S. Food and Drug Administration (FDA) announced the result of a study that examined the risk of suicide among people with epilepsy. The FDA's report stated that patients who took antiepileptic drugs were more than three times as likely to have suicidal thoughts or behavior compared to participants in the study who were given placebos.

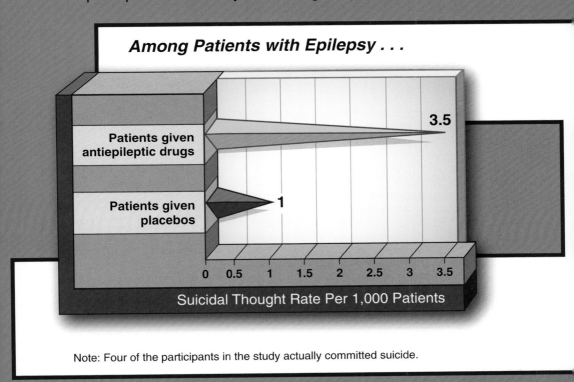

Among Patients with Epilepsy . . .

Patients given antiepileptic drugs — 3.5

Patients given placebos — 1

Suicidal Thought Rate Per 1,000 Patients

0   0.5   1   1.5   2   2.5   3   3.5

Note: Four of the participants in the study actually committed suicide.

Source: U.S. Food and Drug Administration, "Information for Healthcare Professionals: Suicidality and Antiepileptic Drugs," January 31, 2008. www.fda.gov.

- The National Institute for Neurological Disorders and Stroke states that seizures sometimes cause **brain damage**, especially if they are severe.

Can Epilepsy Be Cured?

Because epilepsy is a brain disorder rather than a disease, it cannot be cured in the same way that infectious diseases can be cured with antibiotics, nor can it be prevented with vaccinations. It is a highly complex disorder that does not fit into any one particular category, has many possible contributors but no clearly defined cause, and can strike seemingly healthy children or adults without warning, even if there is no family history of epilepsy. The prognosis for those who suffer from it can differ based on the type of epilepsy, the location in the brain, and the severity of seizures. For many, medications have either stopped seizures altogether or significantly lessened their occurrence. One epilepsy sufferer who stopped having seizures due to medications is Lauren Axelrod. Since she began taking an anticonvulsant drug called Keppra more than nine years ago, she has remained seizure free. According to John M. Pellock, who is a neurologist at Virginia Commonwealth University, antiepileptic drugs help the majority of epilepsy sufferers. He explains: "About two-thirds of seizures can be controlled. It's not a cure—you're not changing long-term outcome, but you can prevent injuries."[43]

Operating on the Brain

Thus far, the only method of curing epilepsy has been brain surgery, during which the abnormal section of the brain is removed. But this is a very serious operation, and the only people who are candidates for it are those for whom medication cannot control seizures and/or for whom the side effects of medication have an adverse impact on their quality of life. Also, surgery is not always an option because in some people, the entire brain is affected rather than one localized area. Dan Wheeless is one epilepsy sufferer who is not a candidate for surgery, as he explains: "I have generalized epilepsy, so it's not in any specific part of the brain, rather than partialized where they can pinpoint it and surgery is an option. For me it's not."[44] For many people who do have partialized seizures, surgery has been successful and has vastly improved their quality of life. According to a study by the Mayo Clinic, 81 percent of patients who underwent brain surgery were either totally or nearly seizure free within 6 months, and 10 years later 72 percent were either seizure free or had a significant reduction in seizures.

In order for surgeons to perform such an operation, they must be able to locate the precise region of the brain that is affected. Accuracy is crucial, as pediatric epilepsy specialist Deborah Holder explains: "We don't want any weakness, any memory problems, any language problems, any vision problems. We don't want to lose anything. So you want to make sure you take out only the area of the brain making the seizures, not any of the brain surrounding it."[45] Researchers have developed sophisticated techniques that help them accurately map the brain. For instance, physicians at Children's Hospital of Pittsburgh use a digital brain wave machine, which uses sensors placed on a child's head and creates a high-tech image of the brain. The patient

> " For many [epilepsy sufferers], medications have either stopped seizures altogether or significantly lessened their occurrence. "

is sedated, then surgeons expose the skull and brain and place electrodes directly on the surface of the brain in order to locate the area where electrical misfires occur. Once they have located the exact region (known as the seizure focus), they are able to cut it out.

One epilepsy sufferer whose life dramatically improved after brain surgery is Anne Marie Hagan, who had her first seizure when she was 40 years old. She was devastated at hearing the epilepsy diagnosis, as she explains:

> There were many mornings when I didn't have the strength to face the outside world. The uncertainty of never knowing when or where the seizures might occur was terrifying. . . . I would often go for a walk, and an hour later wake up out of a daze and find myself in a totally different part of the city having no idea how I got there or what happened along the way. Afterwards, I would often sit on the sidewalk crying, wondering what would become of me. I had never known such vulnerability. My mind and my body were betraying me.[46]

When medication proved ineffective at getting Hagan's seizures under control, her physician suggested that she undergo brain surgery. She was terrified because she was well aware of the substantial risks involved, including stroke, permanent amnesia, and even the possibility of death. She chose to go ahead with it, though, because her seizures were happening more and more frequently and she was miserable. During the operation the surgeon located scar tissue and a large, benign lesion on her brain, and he removed them. She woke up from anesthesia and was relieved to find out that the surgery had been successful, as she explains: "I was very, very blessed that my operation was a complete success . . . and I have been seizure free ever since."[47]

A Radical Brain Operation

From the time Lily Rossignol was two months old, she suffered from severe seizures—in one day alone her tiny body was wracked with 350 of them. She was diagnosed with infantile spasms, which doctors said was caused by a stroke that she suffered before she was born. By the time Lily was 10 months old, her seizures were so severe and happening so frequently that she was at risk of dying. She was so sick that she almost never smiled, laughed, or babbled, nor was she able to sleep. The Rossignols' physician referred them to an epilepsy specialist, who determined that two-thirds of the right hemisphere of Lily's brain was damaged and the only hope of saving her life was a hemispherectomy—an operation that involved removing the entire right half of her brain. According to the specialist, such surgery can be highly effective in young children because of the brain's neuroplasticity, or the ability to rewire itself when it is injured. He explained that when one hemisphere is removed, the void fills with spinal fluid and the other hemisphere takes over the functions of both.

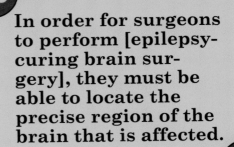

In order for surgeons to perform [epilepsy-curing brain surgery], they must be able to locate the precise region of the brain that is affected.

Lily's parents initially panicked at the thought of having their little girl undergo such radical surgery. They knew there was no other choice, however, so they consented, and Lily had the operation in April 2008. The results were amazing and apparent immediately because she was talking and smiling right after the surgery. "It really, really was like a miracle,"[48] says her father, Paul Rossignol. Five months later, at the age of 16 months, Lily was babbling, smiling, playing with toys, and seemed to be developing normally for her age. Although her parents say that she still faces physical challenges and there are no guarantees about what the future holds, they have every hope that she will fully recover and lead a happy, healthy life.

Seizures Caused by Stress?

Today, with improved surgical techniques and numerous anticonvulsive medications, there is more hope for people with epilepsy than ever before. Yet those treatments do not work for all epilepsy sufferers. Many are not candidates for surgery and have little or no seizure control after taking drugs, which can be a source of frustration as well as despair. Joshua Kors suffered from horrible recurring seizures when he was a teenager, and he says that medication made him feel like a zombie. Formerly a straight-A student, the drugs affected his brain in such a way that he had trouble reading, writing, and paying attention in class. In fact, he began to believe that the side effects were worse than the seizures themselves, and he was starting to feel desperate. "I was on my own, and that made me feel hopeless," he writes. "I woke up each morning afraid of the day's coming seizures. I went to bed, imagining the electricity racing through my frayed neural network, wondering if it would go haywire now. Or now. Or now."[49]

From his mother, Kors heard about the Andrews/Reiter Epilepsy Research Program, an alternative treatment facility in Santa Rosa, California. The cofounders, Donna Andrews and Joel Reiter, have a theory about epilepsy: that in the same way seizures can be triggered by lack of sleep, alcohol, and caffeine, they can also be triggered by stressful emotions such as rage, panic, and worry. During his five-day stay at the facility, Kors was given training in relaxation and deep breathing, and he discussed with Andrews (who is a psychologist) the thoughts and feelings that he had prior to seizures. In those sessions he became aware of patterns he had never recognized before, including stifling his anger when he got mad rather than releasing it. This always happened just before Kors saw the bursts of light, which Andrews informed him were auras. She explained that by focusing on relaxing and deep breathing, he could resolve the tension within himself and potentially avoid having seizures. Today, although he is not 100 percent seizure free, Kors says that what he learned from Andrews and Reiter did wonders for him, and his life is now full and happy.

> " From the time Lily Rossignol was two months old, she suffered from severe seizures—in one day alone her tiny body was wracked with 350 of them. "

The Ketogenic Diet

During the 1920s physicians working with children who had epilepsy made a surprising finding: Their seizures either stopped or were significantly reduced when they were put on short-term "starvation diets" that consisted of nothing but water. They theorized that this was the result of ketosis, a state in which there is a shortage of insulin in the blood and the body starts breaking down its own fat for energy. No one knew why this had an effect on seizures, but scientists became interested in the connection between ketosis and epilepsy. R.M. Wilder, a physician at the Mayo Clinic, theorized that it was possible to produce this same result with a special diet, rather than with fasting, and it would be much safer than prolonged starvation. In 1921 Wilder wrote: "In any case, as has long been known, it is possible to provoke ketogenesis by feeding diets which are very rich in fat and low in carbohydrate. It is proposed therefore, to try the effects of such ketogenic diets on a series of epileptics."[50] Awareness of the ketogenic diet grew over the following de-

> " **Awareness of the ketogenic diet grew over the following decades, although it remained a controversial treatment for epilepsy.** "

cades, although it remained a controversial treatment for epilepsy. Once antiepileptic drugs became available, the diet was rarely used.

During the 1990s there was a resurgence of interest in the ketogenic diet. A television documentary presented the story of two-year-old Charlie Abrahams who suffered from severe, recurring tonic-clonic seizures. Charlie's condition was grave, as his father, Jim Abrahams, explains:

> After thousands of seizures, an incredible array of drugs, dozens of blood draws, eight hospitalizations, a mountain of EEGs, MRIs, CAT scans, and PET scans, one fruitless brain surgery, five pediatric neurologists in three cities, two homeopathists, and countless prayers, Charlie's seizures were unchecked. His development was "delayed," and he had a prognosis of continued seizures and progressive retardation.[51]

While researching epilepsy on his own, Abrahams heard about the ketogenic diet and decided to try it on his son, so the family traveled to the Mayo Clinic so Charlie could start on it under medical supervision. The results seemed miraculous, as Abrahams explains: "Since Christmas, 1993 he has been seizure and drug free . . . and has been off the diet for several years. His favorite song is 'I feel good.'"[52] The Abrahams went on to form the Charlie Foundation, an organization whose mission is to educate people about the effectiveness of the high-fat, low-protein, and low-carbohydrate diet in treating childhood epilepsy.

Although the ketogenic diet was once considered controversial, it has become less so in recent years. The effectiveness of the diet was discussed in a paper that was published in June 2008. British researchers conducted a study that involved 145 children aged 2 to 16 who were having at least 7 seizures a week and had failed to respond to at least 2 antiepileptic drugs. One group began the diet immediately, and the other (the control group) waited 3 months before starting the diet. By the end of the study, 38 percent of the children in the first group saw their seizures reduced by half, with 5 of them having more than 90 percent reduction. In the control group, only 6 percent had significant seizure reduction.

What the Future Holds

Although there is no guaranteed cure for epilepsy, medications, surgical techniques, and alternative treatments have improved the quality of life for numerous epilepsy sufferers. Many have become either seizure free or have seen a significant reduction in seizures after undergoing one or more of these treatments. Researchers continue to study the disorder aggressively in the hope that their discoveries will someday lead to a cure— and for those whose lives are affected by epilepsy, that cannot possibly happen soon enough.

Primary Source Quotes*

Can Epilepsy Be Cured?

"At the moment there is no cure for epilepsy. However, with the right type and dosage of anti-epileptic medication, about 70 per cent of people with epilepsy could have their seizures completely controlled."

—Epilepsy Action, "What Is Epilepsy?" November 2008. www.epilepsy.org.uk.

Epilepsy Action is the largest member-led epilepsy organization in Great Britain.

....

"I am still on minimal medication, but my epilepsy has never returned. Being free from this condition after 53 years has transformed my life."

—Cheryl Jasper, "For 50 Years Cheryl's Life Was Wrecked by Epilepsy—Then She Was Cured by Cutting a Slice from Her Brain," *Daily Mail*, December 9, 2008. www.dailymail.co.uk.

Jasper is a psychotherapist from the United Kingdom who underwent brain surgery to cure her epilepsy.

....

* Editor's Note: While the definition of a primary source can be narrowly or broadly defined, for the purposes of Compact Research, a primary source consists of: 1) results of original research presented by an organization or researcher; 2) eyewitness accounts of events, personal experience, or work experience; 3) first-person editorials offering pundits' opinions; 4) government officials presenting political plans and/or policies; 5) representatives of organizations presenting testimony or policy.

"Antiepileptic drugs do not cure epilepsy; they reduce brain excitability so that seizures are less likely to occur."

—Martha Morrell, "The Falling Sickness Story: A Neurologist's View," *New York Sun*, August 3, 2007. www.nysun.com.

Morrell is clinical professor of neurology at Stanford University.

"Although some childhood epilepsy syndromes tend to go into remission or stop entirely during adolescence, juvenile myoclonic epilepsy is usually present for life once it develops. It can be controlled with medication, but cannot, at this time, be cured."

—Genetic and Rare Diseases Information Center, "Juvenile Myoclonic Epilepsy," January 20, 2009. http://rarediseases. info.nih.gov.

The Genetic and Rare Diseases Information Center, which is an agency of the National Institutes of Health, is dedicated to helping people find useful information about genetic and rare diseases.

"As I pray every night for Gianna's seizures to stop, I also pray for a cure—and for much comfort for the millions of people and their families affected by epilepsy."

—Wendy Flammia, "Gianna's Story," Citizens United for Research in Epilepsy. www.cureepilepsy.org.

Flammia is the mother of a seven-year-old girl who has epilepsy.

"While seizures can be easy to diagnose and control for some people, for many others, epilepsy is a life-long problem that can affect people in many different ways."

—Steven C. Schachter and Patricia O. Shafer, "All About Epilepsy and Seizures," Epilepsy Therapy Project, November 2, 2007. www.epilepsy.com.

Schachter is a professor of neurology at Harvard Medical School, and Shafer is an epilepsy nurse specialist in the Department of Neurology at Boston's Beth Israel Deaconess Medical Center.

66Benign rolandic epilepsy is called 'benign' because it has a good outcome—nearly all children with it will outgrow it during puberty.99

—Richard Appleton, "Benign Rolandic Epilepsy," Epilepsy Action, May 17, 2009. www.epilepsy.org.uk.

Appleton is a neurologist from the United Kingdom who specializes in children's epilepsy.

66Historically, epilepsy has been neglected and misunderstood. This has impeded scientific progress, leaving treatment and research efforts in the dark ages.99

—Citizens United for Research in Epilepsy, "It's Time We Found a Cure," 2008. www.cureepilepsy.org.

Citizens United for Research in Epilepsy is a volunteer-based organization that is dedicated to finding a cure for epilepsy by raising funds for research and increasing awareness of the prevalence and risks of the disorder.

Can Epilepsy Be Cured?

- According to health-care professionals at the Dartmouth-Hitchcock Medical Center, success rates for becoming seizure free following a type of brain surgery known as temporal lobectomy average over **90 percent**.

- The Epilepsy Foundation states that **10 percent** of epilepsy patients fail to gain control of seizures despite trying various types of antiepileptic drugs.

- In May 2009 researchers from Carnegie Mellon University announced that they have identified a new **anticonvulsant compound** that has the potential to stop the development of epilepsy in someone who has a first seizure.

- In May 2008 British researchers announced a study involving children with epilepsy who were fed the high-fat, low-carbohydrate ketogenic diet; **38 percent** of the children had their seizures reduced by half, and 5 of those saw a **90 percent** reduction in seizures.

- According to the New York University Comprehensive Epilepsy Center, more than **90 percent** of children who have epilepsy surgery stop having seizures entirely or have a reduction in the number of seizures.

- Studies have shown that the earlier in a child's development **epilepsy surgery** is performed, the better the outcome.

Brain Surgery as a Cure

Not everyone who has epilepsy is a candidate for surgery. In order for such an operation to be performed, physicians must be able to pinpoint the exact area of the brain where seizures originate (known as the seizure focus), and that is not possible in people who have generalized epilepsy, a type that affects the entire brain. But for those who have localized epilepsy, surgery can markedly improve their quality of life by stopping seizures altogether or significantly reducing their frequency. This illustration shows the result of a brain scan developed by the Mayo Clinic and used to locate seizure "hotspots."

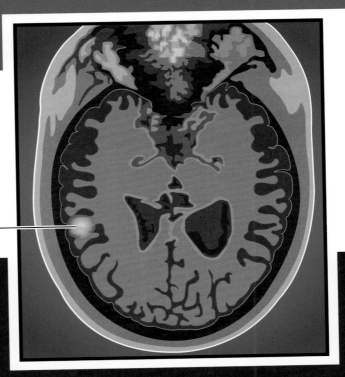

seizure focus

Source: Mayo Clinic, "Epilepsy: Diagnosis," 2009. www.mayoclinic.org.

• The Epilepsy Therapy Project states that infection is the most frequent complication of epilepsy surgery, with the rate of infection being from **1 percent to 2 percent** of patients.

Funding for Epilepsy Research

Although the National Institutes of Health (NIH) allocates money each year for the study of epilepsy, that funding is significantly lower than what is allocated for numerous other diseases and disorders, as this graph illustrates. In 2008, $145 million was allocated for epilepsy as compared to $2.9 billion for HIV/AIDS.

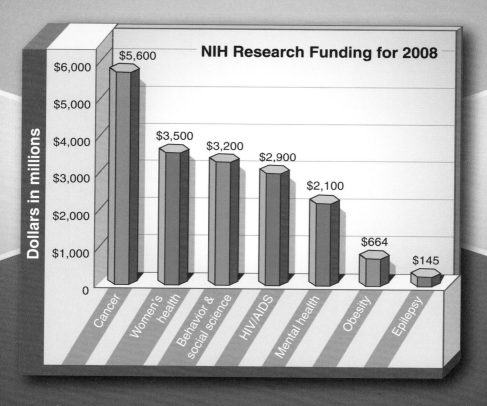

NIH Research Funding for 2008

Source: National Institutes of Health, "Estimates of Funding for Various Research, Condition, and Disease Categories," January 15, 2009. http://report.nih.gov.

- According to a study by the Mayo Clinic, **81 percent** of patients with localized epilepsy who underwent brain surgery were either totally or nearly seizure free within six months.

Vagus Nerve Stimulation

Although it is not a cure, a relatively new type of therapy known as vagus nerve stimulation (VNS) reduces seizures in some epilepsy sufferers by up to 40 percent. Often called a "pacemaker for the brain," VNS involves surgically implanting a silver-dollar-sized generator underneath the skin of the chest. A plastic tube that contains electrodes is threaded under the skin and wrapped around the vagus nerve, one of a pair of nerves in the neck that act as a major connection between the brain and the rest of the body. The surgeon then programs the battery-powered device to deliver small jolts of electricity to the vagus nerve every few minutes. Although scientists are not sure exactly why stimulating the vagus nerve helps reduce seizures, it is thought that it somehow intercepts abnormal brain activity.

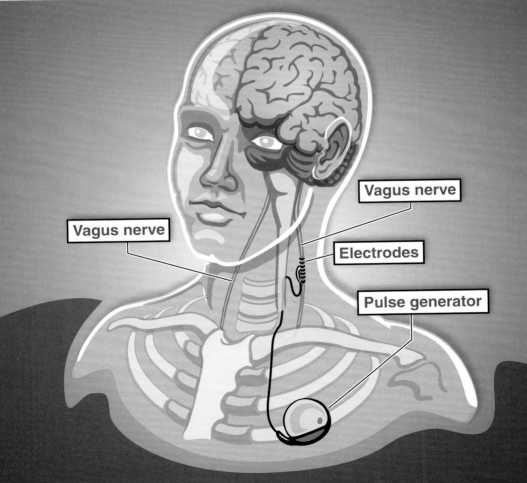

Vagus nerve

Vagus nerve

Electrodes

Pulse generator

Sources: Mayo Clinic, "Epilepsy Treatments and Drugs," April 28, 2009. www.mayoclinic.com; Epilepsy Foundation, "Vagus Nerve Stimulation Therapy," www.epilepsyfoundation.org.

Key People and Advocacy Groups

Susan Axelrod: A woman from Chicago whose 27-year-old daughter has epilepsy and who is known for her commitment to promoting and raising funds for Citizens United for Research in Epilepsy, an organization that she cofounded in 1998.

Hans Berger: A German psychiatrist who developed electroencephalography technology, making it possible to record electrical currents in the brain and graphically depict them on paper.

Centers for Disease Control and Prevention (CDC): An agency of the U.S. Department of Health and Human Services that is charged with promoting health and quality of life by controlling disease, injury, and disability.

Citizens United for Research in Epilepsy (CURE): A volunteer-based organization that is dedicated to finding a cure for epilepsy by raising funds for research and increasing awareness of the prevalence and risks of the disorder.

Raymond Damadian: A physician and scientist who discovered the basis for using magnetic resonance imaging as a tool for medical diagnosis.

Orrin Devinsky: A noted authority on epilepsy who runs the New York University Langone Medical Center, one of the largest epilepsy centers in the country, Devinsky is also a cofounder of the Epilepsy Therapy Project.

Epilepsy Foundation of America: An organization whose mission is to ensure that people with seizures are able to participate in all life experiences; to improve how people with epilepsy are perceived, accepted, and valued in society; and to promote research for a cure.

Epilepsy Therapy Project: An organization that is dedicated to overcoming what it calls the funding gaps and roadblocks that slow the progress of new therapies from the laboratory to the patient.

Michael Gruenthal: A nationally known authority on epilepsy, Gruenthal is the chair of the Department of Neurology at Albany Medical College and codirector of the Neurosciences Institute in Albany, New York.

National Institute for Neurological Disorders and Stroke: An agency that seeks to reduce the burden of neurological disease throughout the world with research and education.

People Against Childhood Epilepsy (PACE): An organization whose focus is on fundraising efforts that support advances in medical research, as well as providing information and support to parents with children who have epilepsy.

Chronology

1956
Seventeen U.S. states have laws in place that forbid people with epilepsy from getting married.

400 B.C.
The Greek physician Hippocrates writes the first book on epilepsy and declares that it is a brain disorder rather than a sign that someone is possessed by demons.

1929
German psychiatrist Hans Berger develops electroencephalography technology, which makes it possible to record electrical currents in the brain and graphically depict them on paper.

1904
American neurologist William Spratling coins the term *epileptologist* to describe someone who specializes in epilepsy.

1900

1930

1960

A.D. 1870
British neurologist John Hughlings Jackson publishes an essay stating that a seizure is a symptom of epilepsy, rather than a disease in and of itself.

1944
Neurologist Frederic A. Gibbs founds the first epilepsy clinic in the United States at the University of Illinois College of Medicine in Chicago.

1968
The Epilepsy Association of America and the Epilepsy Foundation merge to form the Epilepsy Foundation of America.

1912
Two independent teams of chemists create phenobarbital, the first drug for the treatment of epilepsy.

1980
Missouri becomes the last U.S. state to repeal laws that forbid people with epilepsy to marry.

2009
Researchers announce that children born to women who took the antiepileptic medication sodium valproate during pregnancy score lower on IQ tests than those who were not exposed to the drug.

1979
Tony Coelho is the first person with epilepsy to be elected to the U.S. House of Representatives.

1990
Passage of the Americans with Disabilities Act prohibits employers from discriminating against qualified individuals based on disabilities, including those who suffer from epileptic seizures.

1970   1990   2010

2000
The National Institutes of Health launches the nation's first conference on epilepsy.

1978
The National Epilepsy League merges with the Epilepsy Foundation of America.

2005
The daytime program *The Young and the Restless* is the first television show to feature a major character with epilepsy.

2007
The first National Walk for Epilepsy is held in Washington, D.C., to increase awareness about epilepsy, and it becomes an annual event.

2008
Computer hackers break into the Epilepsy Foundation's online forum and imbed JavaScript code and flashing animation, which triggers seizures in some epilepsy sufferers who visit the site.

Related Organizations

American Epilepsy Society (AES)

42 N. Main St.

West Hartford, CT 06117-2507

phone: (860) 586-7505 • fax: (860) 586-7550

Web site: www.aesnet.org

The AES seeks to promote interdisciplinary communications, scientific investigation, and exchange of clinical information about epilepsy. The Web site features fact sheets, news releases, position statements, and research abstracts.

Centers for Disease Control and Prevention (CDC)—Epilepsy

4770 Buford Hwy. NE

MS K-51

Atlanta, GA 30341

phone: (800) 232-4636

e-mail: cdcinfo@cdc.gov • Web site: www.cdc.gov/epilepsy

The CDC, which is part of the U.S. Department of Health and Human Services, is charged with promoting health and quality of life by controlling disease, injury, and disability. This Web site focuses specifically on epilepsy and offers data and statistics, information about research projects, abstracts of various published articles, and a search engine that produces a wide variety of epilepsy-related materials.

Charlie Foundation to Help Cure Pediatric Epilepsy

1223 Wilshire Blvd., Suite 815

Santa Monica, CA 90403

phone:(310) 393-2347 • fax: (310) 453-4585

e-mail: ketoman@aol.com • Web site: www.charliefoundation.org

The Charlie Foundation was founded in 1994 in order to raise awareness about the high-fat, low-carbohydrate ketogenic diet as a treatment for childhood epilepsy, which its Web site claims is more effective than drugs at controlling epilepsy in children with difficult-to-control seizures. Its site features "Charlie's Story," after whom the organization is named; frequently asked questions; numerous articles; a photo gallery; and congressional testimony.

Citizens United for Research in Epilepsy (CURE)

730 N. Franklin St., Suite 404

Chicago, IL 60654

phone: (312) 255-1801 • fax: (312) 255-1809

e-mail: info@cureepilepsy.org • Web site: www.cureepilepsy.org

CURE is a volunteer-based organization that is dedicated to finding a cure for epilepsy by raising funds for research and increasing awareness of the prevalence and risks of the disorder. Its Web site features facts about epilepsy, personal stories, information about research grants, and the newsletter *CURE*.

Epilepsy Foundation of America

8301 Professional Pl.

Landover, MD 20785-7223

phone: (301) 459-3700 • toll-free (800) 332-1000 • fax: (301) 577-2684

e-mail: postmaster@efa.org • Web site: www.epilepsyfoundation.org

The Epilepsy Foundation works to ensure that people with seizures are able to participate in all life experiences; to improve how people with epilepsy are perceived, accepted, and valued in society; and to promote research for a cure. Its Web site features research information, news releases, sections titled "About Epilepsy" and "Living with Epilepsy," and "e-communities" that allow people with epilepsy to chat online.

Epilepsy Institute

257 Park Ave. South, Suite 302

New York, NY 10010

phone: (212) 677-8550 • fax: (212) 677-5825

e-mail: website@epilepsyinstitute.org

Web site: www.epilepsyinstitute.org

The Epilepsy Institute serves people with epilepsy in the New York City area with counseling, vocational services, job placement, coordination of services, information and referral, educational programs, stress management, and other services. Its Web site offers facts about epilepsy (in several languages), frequently asked questions, news and information, and links to other epilepsy organizations.

Epilepsy Therapy Project

PO Box 742

Middleburg, VA 20118

phone: (540) 687-8077 • fax: (540) 687-8066

e-mail: epilepsytherapy@epilepsytherapy.org

Web site: www.epilepsy.com

The Epilepsy Therapy Project is dedicated to overcoming what it calls the funding gaps and roadblocks that slow the progress of new therapies from the laboratory to the patient. Its Web site features an expansive collection of information, such as numerous articles written by medical professionals; an "All About Epilepsy & Seizures" section; special informative areas targeted at kids, teens, women, families, and seniors; and a "My.epilepsy.com Community" with a community forum, groups, blogs, and a chat room.

Mayo Clinic

200 First St. SW

Rochester, MN 55905

phone: (507) 284-2511 • fax: (507) 284-0161

Web site: www.mayoclinic.com

The Mayo Clinic is a medical practice that is dedicated to the diagnosis and treatment of virtually every type of complex illness. Its Web site features a special section on epilepsy, with information about causes, symptoms, risk factors, treatment, lifestyle, home remedies, and a slide show about how the brain works.

National Institute for Neurological Disorders and Stroke (NINDS)

PO Box 5801

Bethesda, MD 20824

phone: (301) 496-5751 • toll-free: (800) 352-9424

fax: (301) 402-2060

Web site: www.ninds.nih.gov

The NINDS, which is part of the National Institutes of Health, seeks to reduce the burden of neurological disease throughout the world with research and education. Its Web site features a section devoted entirely to epilepsy that offers numerous publications, news releases, research findings, and a comprehensive "Seizures and Epilepsy: Hope Through Research" document.

People Against Childhood Epilepsy (PACE)

7 E. Eighty-fifth St., Suite A3

New York, NY 10028

phone: (212) 665-7223 • fax: (212) 327-3075

e-mail: pacenyemail@aol.com • Web site: www.paceusa.org

PACE's focus is on fundraising efforts that support advances in medical research, as well as providing information and support to parents with children who have epilepsy. Its Web site features information about causes, treatment, and major problems associated with epilepsy, as well as a "Recommended Reading" list and a link to the PACE blog.

For Further Research

Books

Thomas R. Brown and Gregory L. Holmes, *Handbook of Epilepsy.* Philadelphia: Lippincott Williams and Wilkins, 2008.

Kathlyn Gay, *Epilepsy: The Ultimate Teen Guide.* Lanham, MD: Scarecrow, 2007.

Kaarkuzhali Babu Krishnamurthy, Deborah T. Combs-Cantrell, and Steven C. Schachter, *Epilepsy in Our Lives: Women Living with Epilepsy.* New York: Oxford University Press, 2008.

Stuart McCallum, *Beyond My Control: One Man's Struggle with Epilepsy, Seizure Surgery and Beyond.* Bloomington, IN: Iuniverse, 2008.

Markus Reuber, Christian E. Elger, and Steven C. Schachter, *Epilepsy Explained: A Book for People Who Want to Know More.* New York: Oxford University Press, 2009.

Steven C. Schachter, ed., *Epilepsy in Our Words: Personal Accounts of Living with Seizures.* New York: Oxford University Press, 2008.

William O. Tatum, Peter W. Kaplan, and Pierre Jallon, *Epilepsy A to Z: A Concise Encyclopedia.* New York: Demos Medical, 2009.

Elaine Wyllie, *Epilepsy: A Cleveland Clinic Guide.* Cleveland, OH: Cleveland Clinic, 2008.

Periodicals

Laura Apel, "Living with Epilepsy, Not Around It," *EP*, November 2008.

Laura Apel and Jan Carter Hollingsworth, "Planning Ahead Can Save the Life of a Child with Epilepsy," *EP*, September 2008.

Rick Bentley, "Epileptic Children Find Hope in Electronic Devices," *Fresno (CA) Bee*, March 3, 2009.

Jennifer Calhoun, "Grateful for Each Day: Family Copes with Boy's Seizure Disorder," *Fayetteville (NC) Observer*, February 9, 2009.

Sarah Goodman, "Epilepsy: Diagnosis and Management," *Practice Nurse*, January 11, 2008.

Melissa Fay Greene, "I Must Save My Child," *Parade*, February 15, 2009.

Jeff Hansel, "Mayo Clinic Innovators Help Advance Treatment," *Rochester (MN) Post-Bulletin*, May 2, 2009.

Joshua Kors, "Inner Vision: Writer Joshua Kors Has Learned to Avoid Seizures by Heeding Their Warning Signs," *Current Science*, a *Weekly Reader* publication, January 23, 2009.

John McCormick, "Well-Connected Advocate Pushes for Epilepsy Aid," *Chicago Tribune*, March 24, 2009.

Mike Stobbe, "Taken During Pregnancy, Epilepsy Drug May Lower Child's IQ," *Toronto Globe & Mail*, April 16, 2009.

Elaine Thompson, "Demystifying the Monster," *Worcester (MA) Telegram & Gazette*, March 10, 2009.

Karen Cimino Wilson, "Epilepsy Part of Life for 'Normal Kid,'" *Concord (NC) Independent Tribune*, March 24, 2009.

Internet Sources

Jerry Adler and Eliza Gray, "In the Grip of the Unknown," *Newsweek*, April 20, 2009. www.newsweek.com/id/193484.

Aliyah Baruchin, "Evidence a High-Fat Diet Works to Treat Epilepsy," *New York Times*, May 6, 2008. www.nytimes.com/2008/05/06/health/research/06epil.html?partner=rssnyt&emc=rss.

Centers for Disease Control and Prevention, "Epilepsy," April 1, 2008. www.cdc.gov/epilepsy.

Jon Meacham, "Epilepsy in America: What Must Be Done," *Newsweek*, April 20, 2009. www.newsweek.com/id/193480.

National Institute of Neurological Disorders and Stroke, "Seizures and Epilepsy: Hope Through Research," April 24, 2009. www.ninds.nih.gov/disorders/epilepsy/detail_epilepsy.htm.

New York Times Health Guide, "Epilepsy," February 11, 2009. http://health.nytimes.com/ref/health/healthguide/esn-epilepsy-ess.html.

Kevin Poulsen, "Hackers Assault Epilepsy Patients via Computer," *Wired*, March 28, 2008. www.wired.com/politics/security/news/2008/03/epilepsy.

Source Notes

Overview

1. Dan Wheeless, "Struggling with Epilepsy," *Newsweek* video, April 2009. http://video.newsweek.com.
2. Wheeless, "Struggling with Epilepsy."
3. Wheeless, "Struggling with Epilepsy."
4. Joshua Kors, "The Talking Treatment: Looking at a New Approach to Epilepsy," JoshuaKors.com, May 2003. www.joshuakors.com.
5. Kors, "The Talking Treatment."
6. National Institute of Neurological Disorders and Stroke, "Seizures and Epilepsy: Hope Through Research," April 24, 2009. www.ninds.nih.gov.
7. Cynthia Folio, "A Self-Portrait by Lydia Thompson: The Essay," Epilepsy Therapy Project, October 17, 2007. www.epilepsy.com.
8. Quoted in Jerry Adler and Eliza Gray, "In the Grip of the Unknown," *Newsweek*, April 20, 2009. www.newsweek.com.
9. Quoted in Adler and Gray, "In the Grip of the Unknown."
10. Stacey Gayle, "Hearing Music Gave Me Seizures," *Cosmopolitan*, August 2008, p. 154.
11. Folio, "A Self-Portrait by Lydia Thompson."
12. Kevin Eggers, interviewed by Laura Apel, "Living with Epilepsy, Not Around It," *EP*, November 2008, p. 48.
13. Quoted in *ScienceDaily*, "Quality of Life Study Examines Burden of Epilepsy," October 30, 2007. www.sciencedaily.com.
14. National Institute of Neurological Disorders and Stroke, "Seizures and Epilepsy."

What Is Epilepsy?

15. Quoted in Stanley Finger, *Minds Behind the Brain*. New York: Oxford University Press, 2000, p. 30.
16. Quoted in Mervyn J. Eadie and Peter F. Bladin, *A Disease Once Sacred: A History of the Medical Understanding of Epilepsy*. Eastleigh, UK: John Libby Eurotext, 2001, p. 140.
17. Quoted in Eadie and Bladin, *A Disease Once Sacred*, p. 142.
18. Quoted in R. Edward Hogan and Kitti Kaiboriboon, "The 'Dreamy State': John Hughlings Jackson's Ideas of Epilepsy and Consciousness," *American Journal of Psychiatry*, October 2003. http://ajp.psychiatryonline.org.
19. National Institute of Neurological Disorders and Stroke, "Seizures and Epilepsy."
20. Quoted in Gregory L. Holmes, "Lennox-Gestaut Syndrome," Epilepsy Therapy Project, February 1, 2004. www.epilepsy.com.
21. Sue Nowak (not her real name), interview with author, May 10, 2009.
22. Nowak, interview.
23. Marta (not her real name), interview with author, May 8, 2009.
24. Marta, interview.
25. Marta, interview.

What Causes Epilepsy?

26. Quoted in Melissa Fay Greene, "I Must Save My Child," *Parade*, February 15, 2009, p. 4.
27. Quoted in Greene, "I Must Save My Child," p. 5.
28. Elizabeth Donner and Berge Minassian, "Genetics of Epilepsy," About Kids Health, January 30, 2006. www.aboutkidshealth.ca.

29. Epilepsy Therapy Project, "Unverricht-Lundborg Disease," March 30, 2005. www.epilepsy.com.

30. José Vega, "The Quick and Dirty About Stroke-Induced Seizures," About.com: Stroke, December 16, 2008. http://stroke.about.com.

31. Richard Appleton, "Gelastic Epilepsy," Epilepsy Action, July 11, 2007. www.epilepsy.org.uk.

32. Quoted in American Academy of Neurology, "Statement of John Booss, MD on Behalf of the American Academy of Neurology Before the Senate Committee on Veterans' Affairs in Support of S. 1233," May 23, 2007. www.aan.com.

33. Linda Nicholson, "Fetal Alcohol Syndrome," Kids Health, June 2008. http://kidshealth.org.

What Are the Risks Associated with Epilepsy?

34. Quoted in Katherine Lee, "Understanding the Effects of Seizures on Children," Everyday Health, March 5, 2009. www.everydayhealth.com.

35. Quoted in Science Daily, "Drops in Blood Oxygen Levels May Be Key to Sudden Death in Some Epilepsy Patients," November 25, 2008. www.sciencedaily.com.

36. Marlene McElligott, "Sudden Unexplained Death in Epilepsy (SUDEP)," Epilepsy Action, April 25, 2009. www.epilepsy.org.uk.

37. Mark Spitz, Frank Lum, and Edward Maa, "Status Epilepticus," WebMD, March 8, 2007. http://emedicine.medscape.com.

38. Quoted in Jenna Martin, "Does Treatment Aggressiveness Affect the Prognosis of Refractory Status Epilepticus?" Epilepsy Foundation, August 3, 2006. www.epilepsyfoundation.org.

39. Quoted in Angela Babb, "Epilepsy Linked to Higher Risk of Drowning," American Academy of Neurology, August 18, 2008. www.aan.com.

40. C. Akos Szabo, "Risk of Fetal Death and Malformation Related to Seizure Medications," *Neurology*, 2006. www.neurology.org.

41. Quoted in Lauren Cox, "Epilepsy Drug Linked to Autism Risk," ABC News, December 2, 2008. http://abcnews.go.com.

42. Quoted in Adler and Gray, "In the Grip of the Unknown."

Can Epilepsy Be Cured?

43. Quoted in Lee, "Understanding the Effects of Seizures on Children."

44. Wheeless, "Struggling with Epilepsy."

45. Quoted in Ivanhoe Broadcast News, "Cure for Epilepsy?" May 2, 2008. www.ivanhoe.com.

46. Anne Marie Hagan, "Developing Epilepsy Took Me on a Beautiful Journey That Changed My Life Forever," Canadian Epilepsy Alliance. www.epilepsymatters.com.

47. Hagan, "Developing Epilepsy Took Me on a Beautiful Journey That Changed My Life Forever."

48. Quoted in *Albuquerque Journal*, "Waking Lily: Toddler's Life-Threatening Epilepsy Treated by Removing Half of Her Brain," September 16, 2008. www.epilepsy.com.

49. Kors, "The Talking Treatment."

50. Quoted in Carl E. Stafstrom and Jong M. Rho, eds., *Epilepsy and the Ketogenic Diet*. Totowa, NJ: Humana, 2004, p. 38.

51. Jim Abrahams, "Charlie's Story," Charlie Foundation, February 19, 2009. www.charliefoundation.org.

52. Abrahams, "Charlie's Story."

List of Illustrations

Index

About the Author

Peggy J. Parks holds a bachelor of science degree from Aquinas College in Grand Rapids, Michigan, where she graduated magna cum laude. She has written more than 80 nonfiction educational books for children and young adults, as well as published her own cookbook called *Welcome Home: Recipes, Memories, and Traditions from the Heart.* Parks lives in Muskegon, Michigan, a town that she says inspires her writing because of its location on the shores of Lake Michigan.